ME:
The Narcissistic American

ME:

The Narcissistic American

Aaron Stern, M.D., Ph.D.

BALLANTINE BOOKS · NEW YORK

Manufactured in the United States of America

First Edition: October 1979
1 2 3 4 5 6 7 8 9 10

Library of Congress Cataloging in Publication Data

Stern, Aaron.
    Me : the narcissistic American.

    1. Narcissism. 2. United States—Social conditions.
3. Violence—United States. 4. Social psychiatry—
United States. I. Title.
BF575.N35S73   1979   301.15'7'0973   79-13623
ISBN 0-345-28186-1

For Bet

The one who made it
possible for me to
experience what this
book is about—loving.

Author's Note

In these times of women's liberation and equal rights, the last thing I want to be accused of is male chauvinism. I am a man, but I do not regard myself as superior to women in any significant way.

I strongly support the movement for equal rights, but it nevertheless has caused certain awkward moments in the language of this land. The reader will note that I often use the terms "man" and "mankind." I mean for them to include us all. Similarly, when I refer to an infant as "he," it is only because I need to use "her" for "mother" and wish to avoid the possibility of any confusion between the two.

My concern in this book is for all mankind. Mankind, as any good dictionary will inform you, is a word that includes all human beings collectively: men and women.

Contents

Introduction

No society has ever survived success. The record of history is clear.

The Roman Empire provides a richly detailed description of the decline of a great society. The symptoms of its fall centered around a critical schism between the older and younger generations. It was reflected among the young by an increase in drug usage, by a growing experimentation in homosexuality and bisexuality, and, perhaps most symptomatic of all, by a strident demand for more leisure that was accompanied by an unwillingness to accept responsibility for government, family, and other social institutions.

It is all achingly familiar. American society has all these symptoms of terminal disease and more. We are paying the price for success and it is a heavy price indeed, for it could mean the eventual destruction of our society.

Historically, man has fared well when he has been primarily preoccupied with the struggle for survival. The western frontier of a century ago and, in many ways, China today are classic examples. When man is struggling merely to survive, choices are virtually made for him; he does what he must in order to live. He

1

becomes accustomed to a life dominated by a gray reality, a life that permits only fleeting moments in the sun.

When the security of survival is attained, it provides man—and society—with time to pause and ponder the meaning of life. He begins to search for purpose and, as a part of purpose, pleasure. He begins seeking more of those special moments in the sun.

Survival requires adaptation to nature. It is not a simple task. To survive is an accomplishment in its own right. It is characteristic of man, however, not to be satisfied with such an accomplishment alone. Indeed, it is his special arrogance to set out to conquer nature. In this quest, one of the things he most needs to do is to defeat the inevitability of his own mortality, to control the major uncertainty we all face: death.

With the pursuit of immortality comes the invention of rituals, ranging from religion to jogging. For instance, learning that jogging three miles a day improves cardiovascular activity, which, in turn, prolongs life, man decides that thirteen miles would be even better. He seeks—and believes he can attain—the body and constitution of a man twenty years younger in order to defeat the inevitable: aging. And in his desperate attempts to deny the impact of time on his body, he ignores the respect and serenity once associated with growing old.

Man's frustration with the impossibility of conquering nature leads him to challenge the familiar institutions through which he was previously able to survive. Marriage, once the most sacred institution in Western —and Eastern—societies, has steadily been eroded in the quest for more immediate forms of pleasure. Marital union once offered companionship, security, and the foundation on which the most personal society of all was built: the family. Now the divorce rate soars and people want new freedoms. Some advocate the concept of open marriage and all the various forms of

sexual and philosophical promiscuity. We want intimacy without vulnerability, love without commitment
or responsibility.

Our language also reflects this declining state of our
society. Don't express feelings, stay aloof, and, above
all, don't confront choice. These attitudes become
social goals, goals that ingrain themselves in our speech.
"Hang loose," we say. "Stay cool." We admire those
we know who are "laid back" and "do their own
thing."

We seek freedom at all costs but without understanding that freedom is the right to make any choice
we elect, provided we are always willing to pay the
price for that choice.

Today we avoid choice. We avoid committing ourselves to specific long-term goals. We are unable to
sacrifice immediate pleasure for future satisfaction and
fulfillment. We search for some device that will make
choice unnecessary. We want ends without means,
ends without making choices. And what we want, we
want immediately. Delay cannot be tolerated.

For instance, in the service of our need for immediate gratification we invent therapies whose sole inten-
tion is to give instant rebirth with a minimum of effort.
Adults crawl into big cribs and scream away their
troubles—or so they want to believe. We attend group
encounters in the nude or involve ourselves in marathon
adventures oriented to the power of positive thinking,
and on and on. Transcendental this, transactional that,
fill our vocabulary, but do these methods satisfy our
needs? Of course not. Why should they? Has happiness
ever been easy and quick? Because we want it to be
does not mean that it is.

When something is all bad we move away from it.
If it is all good we move toward it. Rarely, if ever, are
human situations this simplistic. Almost everything is
a combination of good and bad. We must make

3

choices. We must give up some good to avoid the bad, and accept some of the bad to retain the good.

The quest for immediate satisfaction is the sure road to the destruction of society. The only alternative to this is to make choices. For human beings to be able to achieve ultimate pleasure and satisfaction, the capacity for making choices is critical. Struggle against this however we will, the situation will never change. The fact is that choice is the highest level of human functioning.

The United States is now sailing unsteadily in the wake of a level of success unmatched in the history of mankind, a success that goes far beyond the mere mechanics of affluence and pleasure. We have become the narcissistic society.

By virtue of all we have learned about human behavior, it is possible for us to understand the erosion of our society. We know the symptoms. What the ancient Romans could not understand about their fate, we can. They could describe their plight, but they could not understand the internal dynamics that brought on the collapse of their society. We can. They could not make the choices we can—and must—if we are to survive.

Relative to our ultimate fate, there are two alternatives. We can permit ourselves to go the way other societies have gone before us, ignoring our understanding. Or we can *choose* to do something about it.

To do something about our destiny, we must understand the nature of narcissism. Why does it follow in the wake of success? How is it experienced individually by each of us and collectively as a society? What do years of study of the behavioral sciences tell us? How can we choose to avert the destruction of our society?

Narcissism is a universal human force. Uncontrolled and improperly channeled, it destroys love between human beings and prohibits the joy we all desire for ourselves and others. Effectively controlled and com-

4

bined with the capacity to care for others—to give of oneself with a genuine purpose—it becomes the spice of life. Whether we control it or it controls us is to me the most crucial choice one can make in a lifetime. Defining, understanding, and exploring this most important choice is the subject of this book.

We are, after all, each and every one of us—beginning with the moment of our birth—narcissists.

1 /

The Human Condition

Man is not born with a capacity to love others. At birth the human infant is essentially a self-centered animal with no interest in or awareness of objects outside himself. His world contains but one inhabitant. Within this singular world he is governed solely by a drive to do his own thing, to fulfill his every need. Immediately.

He enters the world with an omnipotent illusion of total self-fulfillment. When a baby cries from hunger, he does not recognize that it is his mother's breast that provides nourishment and comfort. He simply attributes the removal of the discomfort created by his hunger to the magical power of his cry. Similarly, when his soiled diaper is changed by others to make him more comfortable, he believes he has made it happen.

The newborn child acknowledges only his own existence. He has no concern about whom he awakens in the middle of the night, no concern over displacing other siblings in the family, no concern about demanding maximum attention for himself at the expense of others. Even after being tended by his caring mother, he can make her disappear by merely closing his eyes— or so he thinks.

Each of us becomes capable of loving another only to the extent that he is able to move away from the natural state of total self-absorption he carries into the world from the moment he is born. This exclusive preoccupation with one's self has been labeled by behavioral scientists as narcissism. The word is derived from ancient Greek mythology; it relates to the story of Narcissus, who achieved pleasure by admiring his own reflected image.

The capacity to love another must be learned by human beings. This is no easy task, since loving is in direct opposition to the narcissism that naturally exists at birth. To be able to love, we must learn to neutralize and redirect our narcissistic needs.

In his first months of life, the infant is permitted relatively free self-expression. He sleeps whenever he wishes and eats whenever the need for nourishment arises within him. There is no initial pressure to discriminate day from night or to reserve sleep for the evening hours. He is not expected to regulate his feeding pattern to conform to established mealtimes for breakfast, lunch, or dinner. He empties his bladder and bowels at will. He begins life by regulating his own behavior and leaves it for others to adapt to his set of internal schedules.

Soon that freedom comes into conflict with other members of the family. The needs of others are slowly imposed on him. His self-demand feeding schedule is gradually manipulated by his parents to fit into their daily pattern of eating. He is trained to sleep when they sleep. Restraints are progressively placed on him and his self-centered life style.

As he develops motor skills, his physical movements require external control. As he inches his way to the top of the stairs, his mother gently pulls him back into the safety of the room. As he reaches for the hot oven door, his mother's exclamation and quick movement prevent him from injury. When he grabs for the ex-

8

pensive bric-a-brac, it is hastily moved out of his grasp. As he playfully smears his food, it is taken from him.

Over and over again he is confronted with the frustrating reality that he alone does not control his every wish and move. He is forced to recognize the existence of others, who continually thwart his self-given right to do what he wants when he wants to. But his sense of helpless frustration steadily increases, until finally it stimulates the need to communicate with others, first by a series of grunts and gestures and finally by the beginnings of language. Initially, all attempts at communication are designed to manipulate others into getting for him what he cannot get for himself. He has no interest in others except for what they can do for him.

This recognition of the existence of others and the need to communicate with them represents the first alteration in his narcissistic disposition.

The dependent vulnerability of the infant is the avenue through which his parents establish a relationship with him. From the earliest moments of his life an almost endless variety of techniques are utilized to engage the baby in a dependent attachment to his parents. Countless nurturing parental acts are employed to establish a critical level of dependency that will compel the child to view his parents as vital to his own personal survival. This dependent tie to the parents is the foundation on which the ability to love another person is built.

Through the effective use of mothering, the child is brought to experience another human being. This is constantly reinforced by repeated encounters with his mother. As his need for her evolves, it serves to limit his omnipotence. He is still far removed from any capacity for loving, but he has at least come to a transitional point of needing someone outside himself.

The narcissistic infant is not without guile. His sense of omnipotence may be tarnished, but it is not lost. He will give up only what he must. His mind transforms his mother into a tool, an extension of his omnipotent needs. She has no meaning as a person in her own right and functions only to serve his needs.

Nor is the mother without guile. She persists at making him aware of her ground rules. She scolds when she finds a soiled diaper and plunks her puzzled opponent on a cold toilet seat. She restrains his exploration of forbidden territory with a commanding prohibition. If that fails, she incarcerates him in the confines of a playpen. His nap time is her rest period; and, tired or not, he must lie in his crib, his howls of protest no longer able to accomplish omnipotent feats.

This constant combat resolves itself into an ongoing negotiation, each side demanding concessions for anything that is relinquished. For the parent, it is a system of reward and punishment. Retain your inconsiderate narcissistic ways and be punished; give them up and be rewarded. For the child, it is a constant testing of parentally imposed limits in an effort to retain as much of his narcissism as possible.

The child thus embarks on a lifelong struggle to gratify his needs, learning to be considerate of other human beings while he strives to retain his self-contained narcissism.

The parents engage him in battle by gradually taking away his freedom and returning it piecemeal in exchange for evidence of his submission to their needs. In this way the child learns self-denial, which means that ultimately the majority of his actions will reflect concern for the parents' wishes. Thus the child begins to shift from a primarily narcissistic human being to a social person aware of the existence and needs of others.

Childhood functions as a period during which the child is taught to suppress his natural narcissistic instincts. But it takes work, both on the part of the parents and on that of the child. In the service of this goal, childhood is a uniquely appropriate time to experience deprivation and disappointment. It is ideally designed to permit failure, because then the impact of failing is less damaging than during the adult years. Breaking an expensive toy or taking the wrong mathematics course is far less self-destructive than choosing the wrong mate or pursuing the wrong career later on. It is only by exposure to some failure that the child is able to come to terms with his limitations.

When parents structure childhood exclusively as an adventure in winning, they foster omnipotent behavior —and thus fix the child's narcissism. In the absence of adequate amounts of frustration, the child retains his narcissistic commitment, which will seriously undermine his potential to love as an adult.

When that potential is allowed to develop normally, a critical shift occurs around the third year of life. It is characterized by the child's preoccupation with seeking the love and approval of the parent of the opposite sex. This behavior was initially observed and described by Sigmund Freud, who labeled it the "Oedipus complex." In Greek mythology, Oedipus was sexually attracted to his mother.

Unfortunately, the emphasis on the sexual attraction between a child and the parent of the opposite sex has distorted the significance of this developmental accomplishment, which is that it serves as the first occasion in the child's life when he has sufficiently compromised his narcissism so as to care deeply about another human being.

It is a healthy sign in the child's progression from a narcissistic to a loving person. Reaching the oedipal phase of development does not ensure a life structured around loving, but it is a step in the right direction. The capacity to love will continue to evolve to the extent that the child's narcissistic impulses continue to be neutralized and redirected. In a word: controlled.

Psychiatrists regard any person whose behavior remains fixed at a pre-oedipal level of development—or, for that matter, anyone who regresses to a predominant behavior pattern that is pre-oedipal—as an essentially narcissistic individual. Such a person can care for other human beings only to the extent that they directly serve to provide him with self-gratification. He enjoys the company of others only if it does not compromise his personal needs. He possesses a low tolerance for deprivation and structures his life so that he does not have to endure frustration. He competes only as long as he feels he is winning. He shelters himself from the threat of competitive defeat by participating only in carefully selected activities. He compensates for frustration by frequent withdrawal into fantasy, where there is no limit to his successes. He lives as exclusively as possible to satisfy only his own real and imagined needs, and he tends to them religiously.

Excessive narcissism is at the heart of mental illness. Schizophrenia, the most malignant psychological condition known to man, is defined as a narcissistic disorder. Some experts regard it as a single-disease entity, others as a syndrome that can be produced by many different diseases. All, however, agree that it is characterized by a narcissistic disposition.

Schizophrenia is classified as a psychosis. Psychoses constitute the more severe forms of mental disorders. They are distinguished by a predominant core of self-interest, reflecting an inability to utilize the major sources of one's energies to love another human being. All psychoses, not just schizophrenia, are regarded as narcissistic conditions.

How can one rate one's self in terms of narcissistic behavior? By birthright it is a component of all of us, differing from person to person only in degree. It ranges from the malignant form expressed in psychoses to the benign narcissistic acts that take place in all our lives—even among the best adjusted. None of us— even the most disturbed—are governed absolutely by narcissistic behavior. Nor are any of us totally free of it.

To define one's position in the spectrum of narcissistic behavior, it is useful to imagine a scale extending from zero to one hundred, with zero as an absolute and total narcissism, and one hundred as a completely loving posture devoid of any narcissistic traces. One can then examine all the facets of one's behavior in order to determine what percentage of his actions is exclusively self-fulfilling compared with acts that involve some self-deprivation in the cause of caring about others. Anyone whose life is governed by the forces of narcissism more than fifty percent of the time can be theoretically regarded as primarily narcissistic. A person whose choices reflect the capacity to care for others more than fifty percent of the time would be a primarily loving human being.

Human behavior cannot be easily classified to fit such a scale, and great professional skill would be required to make the necessary judgments regarding the behavior of other human beings. It is possible, however, for each of us to determine for himself whether his behavior is characterized by a predominance of loving others or by narcissistic love. This requires questioning one's motives and examining them relative to one's behavior. Those of us who are primarily narcissistic live a life dominated by the determination to pay little or no price for our actions. The loving person, on the other hand, is prepared to pay the price inherent in his or her choices.

Narcissism and the capacity to love are directly related to each other. As one element increases, inevitably the other must decrease. The more narcissistic one is, the less he can love, and vice versa. But no human being is absolutely capable of loving others. Narcissistic drives are always getting in the way. One can only love in relative terms.

The struggle to prevent our narcissistic selves from overwhelming our caring selves is an enduring one. It is man's fate. It begins at birth and continues to the moment of his death. In the best of circumstances it is an inherent human weakness that is always difficult to overcome.

2 /

The Price of Social Security

The origins of society are rooted in the needs of the weak. Historically, weaker men had no way of protecting the things that were important to them. Their fate was determined solely by the whim of those who were more powerful. Their food, lodgings, and women were available to the strong, simply for the taking. This pattern is consistent with man's evolution as described by Darwin. Like the lower animal forms from which we evolved, the fate of the human animal was determined by the natural process of selection, the survival of the fittest.

Inevitably, it followed that the weak would band together to protect themselves collectively from the strong. They created the beginnings of social order to neutralize the overwhelming power of the strongest among them. They joined together to police the actions of the more powerful so that they could gain more security—and more pleasure—for themselves. Their behavior did not stem from any altruistic motives. The weak framed the beginnings of social order to make it possible for those other than the naturally selected strong to survive. It was an ingenious insurance pro-

15

gram designed to protect each individual from his relative weakness.

For thousands of years man has elaborated on these early social structures. The design, however, has remained basically the same: a system of interdependence that serves to buttress the great majority of us who cannot survive on our own.

Society permits individual members to depend on one another. This interdependence allows each of us to supplement himself. It provides a complicated and intricate system that enables us to compensate for our unique weaknesses by drawing on the strengths of others. We no longer need to grow our own vegetables or hunt for our own food. Supermarkets exist for this purpose. Armies and police forces are employed to protect us from external attack. Physicians are available to ensure our longevity; legal services exist to help us protect what we have come to assume are our individual rights. Political structures have emerged to administer the social system of our choice. Religions have been created by us to serve as moral and social arbiters, and as a method of dealing with the uncertainty of death.

But not without a price! In life there is nothing for nothing. While society does succeed in protecting longevity and providing us with security from external dangers, it also demands great compromises. In exchange for the decrease in external threats, society creates an overwhelming increase in internal tension. Socialization requires us to suppress our natural desires for self-fulfillment and to give up personal freedoms.

In moving from a narcissistic human being to a social animal, man is held·within one of the most prolonged periods of helplessness in the entire animal kingdom; his childhood. By virtue of his dependent state, the child becomes vulnerable to the frustrating, intrusive actions of his parents, who service his helplessness in exchange for initiation into their social club. He is taught to deny the spontaneous flow of his inner direction and is required to resist the great forces within him seeking pleasurable self-expression. Once socialization is achieved, the child is no longer free to express his internal drives directly. Instead, he has learned to live in a constant state of conflict, varying in degree from moment to moment.

The battleground shifts from the outer world to the inner world. This distortion of our natural narcissism splits our being into two conflicting states, reflected in separate "inner" and "outer" faces. The inner face is made up of the multitude of drives and hungers that constitute our innate narcissism. The outer face reveals only those forms of self-expression that have been taught to us as socially acceptable. This shift, and the stress it causes, are the dues we pay for membership in society.

For example, we have all had the experience of responding with rage when someone suddenly cuts us off while we are driving. Our inner face would like to demolish the other vehicle and kill the driver. The outer face permits only the sounding of our horn and a stream of expletives shouted in solitude in our own car.

The distortion of our inner face by the imposed outer face is what the medical profession calls a neurosis. The existence of a neurosis reveals that an individual has learned his lessons well during his childhood; that he has been educated to resist the momentum of his innate narcissism. It substantiates the fact that he has effectively developed a working relationship with his parents and has grown to expand the potential for caring about another human being. Indeed, it is as a consequence of learning to love another that a neurosis is formed. A neurosis is positive proof that a human being has learned to significantly compromise his capacity for narcissistic pleasure. It is the residue of living with superimposed restraints by virtue of concern for other people.

In and of itself, neurosis is not an illness. In fact, it constitutes the highest level of human adjustment within a social structure. If anything, it represents a relatively high state of achievement for any human being. The perhaps surprising fact is that one must first attain a primarily loving orientation toward life before he can be classified as a neurotic.

Neurosis is the price of socialization. One cannot be a social animal without some neurotic behavior. Neurotic conflict is rooted in the loss of freedom imposed on us in the process of converting a totally narcissistic infant into a member of society with a capacity for caring about others, which is the forerunner of the ability to love. This capacity begins with the strong restraints placed first on an infant by his parents and then on an adult by himself.

The restraints imposed on us during childhood are always exaggerated in nature. As we grow and accumulate more skills, it is essential that we constantly re-examine and re-evaluate those restraints. If childhood prohibitions are permitted to persist, they can excessively restrict our adult lives. Adults should be able to tolerate the dark without panic and be alone in an apartment without fear of bodily harm. Similarly, while sexual curiosity could not be openly expressed in childhood, it is too crucial to our well-being for it to be suppressed in adulthood.

Initially the outer face we are taught to develop by our parents is shaped in direct opposition to our inner face. We comply because our early helplessness drives us to submit excessively to the parental forces that both nurture and restrain us. So we start out with a great gap between our inner and outer faces.

The challenge in growing up is to reduce the size of that gap—to be able to satisfy our narcissistic pleasures within the limits of the rules and regulations prescribed by social living. If I am sexually excited by the beautiful wife of my neighbor, I cannot drag her off against her will to satisfy my sexual drives. The fantasy of making love to her, however, can be incorporated into lovemaking with another consenting partner. Maturity should bring with it the freedom to recognize and record our narcissistic interests in pleasure of all forms, along with the ability to pursue those pleasures selectively, in socially acceptable ways. Thus, as adults, we can close the gap between our inner and outer faces. The demands inherent in social living make it impossible for the two faces to coincide exactly, but the closer the two become, the less conflict pervades the life of the adult and the greater is his potential for pleasure within the confines of his socially produced neuroses.

Each person differs with regard to the extent that he is able to find pleasure while burdened by the superimposed maze of restraints that constitutes his individual form of neurosis. It follows, then, that there will be a wide range of self-expression among neurotic people. For some, the inhibiting forces are so severe that expressive action is almost totally subordinated to the dictates of social reality. This is the case with our friend Caspar Milquetoast, who never crosses the street against the lights, never forgets his rubbers and umbrella on a rainy day, never speaks unless he is spoken to, and always has the exact fare ready and in hand when he boards the bus. The only part of himself that he reveals is what others expect of him. His inner face is almost totally subdued by his outer face.

There are those who are even worse off than our friend Caspar Milquetoast. He scrupulously polices and guards his every action, but at least leaves himself the right to a rich fantasy life. He has to obey all the rules in carrying out his deeds, but in the privacy of his thoughts there are no rules. But there are some people who require purity of mind as well as of body.

For them, just the thought of crossing against the light is equivalent to the act of jaywalking. They must police every idea as scrupulously as they police every action. Not only can't they drag off the neighbor's wife to whom they are sexually attracted, they can't even permit themselves to know they are attracted in the first place. The demands for total purity required by their outer face leave no significant room for pleasure. They seek to deny totally the existence of the inner face.

Between the two neurotic extremes—the excessively restrained who live almost devoid of pleasure, and the more autonomous neurotic who lives close to the edge of narcissistic expression—each of us wages a day-by-day lifetime battle. If our quest for pleasure is excessive, we run the risk of being overwhelmed by our narcissistic inner face. If our quest for pleasure is insufficient, we face a life in which we struggle to find meaning or purpose.

The narcissistic state is the natural human condition, constantly threatening to break through and regain its domination over each of us. The superimposed veneer of our outer face is continually under siege. After we achieve the first level of human growth, which enables us to become part of society, a second struggle begins. It is the unending effort to remain a part of society and yet find life worth living in terms of attaining enough pleasure without reverting to a primarily narcissistic state.

The closer we get to such a narcissistic state, the less able we are to tolerate conflict. We become increasingly unwilling to deny ourselves. We experience less internal pain because of a diminished concern for others. The internal neurotic battleground becomes subordinated to the fight against external restraints. We are only momentarily willing to accept compromise. We lose much of our capacity for loving. We seek so much from life that the inevitability of frustration is a constant threat. Our insatiable hungers are so great that the slightest frustration can create the most intense pain, which often leads to depression. The more narcissistic among us are always just around the corner from their next depression.

To maintain our capacity to love, we must hold on to our social commitment. The price we pay for this is neurosis. Loving provides us with the best form of sustaining pleasure within a social context, but it is possible only as long as narcissism is successfully restrained. It is the means by which societies survive.

3 /

From Survival to Loving:
The Family

The success or failure of our society to create loving human beings begins with the smaller society of the family. This basic social structure serves as a microcosm of the world into which we grow as adults. Its effectiveness will ultimately be measured by the degree to which each of us becomes a loving adult. Consequently, failure or success as caring human beings is contained within the unit of the family.

The family constitutes the first society to which each of us must learn to accommodate himself. In addition to its biological connection, it functions as a social institution, with rules, regulations, ethical and moral values, learned habit patterns, and unique physical surroundings. Our earliest—and in many ways strongest—impressions about life are derived as youngsters from our individual families.

No society has ever existed without some form of family structure as the focal point. It is absolutely essential to the perpetuation of social order. Its principal purpose is to provide the means for indoctrinating a child into a social format. This basic task is accomplished through the integration of dependent ties.

It is within the structure of the family that parents

strive to provide their infants with nurturing, which will cause the child to view them as objects essential to his survival. The sophisticated and highly organized bartering system between parent and child takes form in the home. The child struggles to get everything he wants when he wants it, while the parents progressively place restraints on these demands, forcing him to realize he has no other feasible choice than to accept compromised self-expression. He is made to recognize the inevitability of frustration in trying to gain his own ends on his own terms.

Nurturing is the reward for this sacrifice. His helplessness is compensated by his parents' ability to provide for him. This is the beginning of caring, the core of the exchange between parent and child.

His spontaneous drive for pleasure is thus subordinated to the parental demands for social adjustment. The internal pain caused by this conflict trains him to police his behavior. He must learn to develop an elaborate alarm system that will constantly monitor his drives. He must filter all of his actions through an imposed screen of familial ground rules.

If parental deprivation is excessive, the child will not be adequately motivated to give up his own wants to meet the needs of others. In the case of the financially underprivileged, for example, where both parents are forced to work, the child is often left to be part of a pool of similar children who are watched over by an older or disabled woman who can no longer find employment. Such a child can feel emotionally abandoned and come to regard his survival only in terms of his own personal resources, forming no real ties to the family. Cheated by poverty out of the opportunity to develop meaningful, dependent, caring attachments, the child is destined to remain relegated to a life in which he is singularly dedicated to his personal gratification. He will develop no caring, interpersonal relationships. He will feel no responsibility to others, and consequently, no feelings of guilt will plague his daily existence. He will be a person who cannot function meaningfully in society.

One need not be poor to be underprivileged. The overindulged child is also deprived. By virtue of excessive nurturing, he is cheated out of sustained periods of deprivation that are essential if his narcissism is to be redirected. He, too, faces a life of narcissistic perversion.

Once initiated into society through our families, where do we turn to find meaning and purpose for all the years yet to come? Once we have given up our inborn movement toward gratification and pleasure, what substitutes can be found to fill the void?

Nurturing isn't enough. Being guaranteed survival isn't enough. There must be more to life. What makes the restraints imposed on us by society worthwhile? How do we find some way back to a pleasurable form of self-expression? What alternative does society offer?

Loving.

Like everything else in the conflicting state imposed by society, however, loving is not easy to come by— and is available in relative terms at best. All of us must learn to pursue it in our own way, tethered as we are by the biological restraints of our individual makeup.

The paradox about loving is that although its origin is in nurturing, the extent to which we need another person for our self-survival is the extent to which we are limited in our capacity to love that person. Loving requires autonomy and is based on the ability to share one's self with another out of choice, as opposed to dependent need. The more we need someone to protect us in order to ensure survival, the more we are apt to substitute some form of mothering—dependency, nurturing—for mature loving. The highest form of loving is that which exists between two individuals who are capable of separately sustaining themselves.

Dependency acts to suffocate loving. Dependent people feed off one another by virtue of their needs. They live together because they do not have the strength to live alone. They substitute dependent self-fulfillment for sharing, giving themselves the illusion that they are sharing when in fact they are not. They are not free to come and go within the confines of a loving relationship. They are committed to stay by virtue of their inability to make it on their own. They perpetuate the relationship because it functions to fulfill their self-centered interest. Their dependent weakness limits the extent to which they can act out of a loving concern for another. Their excessive requirement for protection limits the extent to which they can subordinate their own self-interest in giving to others.

Only independent people can choose to remain in a relationship. Dependent people remain out of necessity. The most mature level of love exists only in the face of free choice. Therefore, loving can be experienced and enjoyed only to the extent that the participants are able to maintain themselves independently.

Examine our plight. We are born narcissistically free, unencumbered by social demands. However, our helplessness seriously compromises our chances for survival. We opt for survival by giving up the pleasure of uninhibited self-expression for a restrained life style taught to us by our families. As we become secure we begin to search for meaning and purpose. Then comes Catch-22. We learn that the way out is through loving. But in order to effectively reap the harvest of loving, we must be autonomous, independent human beings. Loving is the way out only because we became dependent animals in the first place. Had we not submitted to the restraint of our narcissism, we would have had no special need for loving. The submission, however, was predicated on indoctrinated dependency

—the very force that blocks our way to get where we want to go: the ability to love.

The family has made us social. It has also made us dependent. How do we kick that habit—the addictive bonds of dependent insecurity—so as to become more autonomous and thereby capable of mature love?

As human animals, we derive our strength both from within and from without. The mature human being can shift this balance to the point where most of his strengths come from within, which permits him to accept the insecurity that arises from his vulnerability. His sense of self-esteem gives him confidence to deal with the unexpected and unforeseen. He can tolerate the intimacy of loving because for him surviving does not depend on controlling another.

On the other hand, the person whose strength comes primarily from without must seek to control the outside forces in order to ensure that they constantly work for him and not against him. He is the dependent human being, adopting postures of ingratiation to be sure that others love him—a way of neutralizing his fears of abandonment and isolation. This follows in the wake of his conviction that he cannot survive as a separate individual. He must be able to control his outer face in order to manipulate others into fulfilling his need for security. This constant effort to win the support and approval of others is a hell of a way to go through life—never being able to be one's self for fear of possible rejection. It leaves little margin for loving.

All of us know the good-natured Sams who are "always willing and always cooperative." They never refuse to see the movie you prefer to see, even if they have already seen the picture. They never refuse to eat at the restaurant of your choice, even if it is a little too expensive for them and they don't particularly like the food. Our friend Sam is usually the first to volunteer to run an errand, carry out a dirty chore, give someone a lift in his automobile even if the destination is out of his way, or offer his apartment for the next party. How sad that he is afraid to exist as a real person. How sad that he will not be able to let someone love him for himself.

Becoming a physically mature individual is not a difficult task. It occurs merely by passively flowing with the forces of nature as we grow older. Little is required other than survival. The innate forces that program our physical growth and development will bring about changes in our external appearance—there is little doubt that each of us will grow large enough to be forced to pay adult admission prices at the movies and full fare on airlines.

But emotional maturity does not evolve naturally from inner forces. On the contrary, it requires great effort. Whereas survival guarantees physical maturity for all, it ensures emotional maturity for none.

To attain emotional maturity, each of us must learn to develop two critical capacities: the ability to live with uncertainty and the ability to delay immediate gratification in favor of long-range goals.

To live with uncertainty, we must come to terms with the inevitability of death and the unpredictable moment of its arrival.

As children, we seek mastery over the external forces that contribute to our fate. The Superman and Superwoman fantasies that each of us enjoys in his lifetime are residuals of infantile magical wishes for supernatural powers. The desire for total control over one's body is a universal human phenomenon most commonly expressed in man's pursuit of immortality.

We live in constant fear of death. We have difficulty in accepting the mortal limits of our own physical dimensions. We attempt to resolve this temporary existence through religious beliefs in an immortal hereafter. While inhabiting the earth, some of us strive relentlessly to ensure that traces of our existence will remain after our death. Thus, some work to accumulate large sums of money that can be perpetuated into a name-bearing, self-sustaining, ongoing estate. Others seek recognition through historical records like a national monument or a bust in the Hall of Fame.

Should celebrated fame escape us, we nevertheless have the means of propagating the fantasy of immortality through our children. The existence of a child provides the parent with a narcissistic extension of himself.

For Shakespeare, the coward dies many deaths, the brave man only one. I would paraphrase this to mean that the insecure, frightened man who cannot accept the uncertainties inherent in living finds little pleasure in life because he is constantly plagued by his fear of death. Man must accept death in order to enjoy life.

Only by accepting the reality of uncertainty can we find more pleasure in living. As Auntie Mame said, life is a banquet, but most sons of bitches are too frightened to sit down and eat.

Man must acknowledge that he has very limited control over the forces relating to his life. We humans must accept our mortality and relative insignificance in the total scheme of the universe. Those who are unable to accept this limitation go through life generating self-deceptive thoughts to create illusions of omnipotence and immortality. On the other hand, those who do accept vulnerability to uncertainty as a constant have a shot at sitting down at the banquet of life and consuming whole meals of happiness.

The second quality we must attain to develop our potential for loving is the capacity to delay immediate gratification in favor of longer-term goals. Characteristically, a child wants what he wants when he wants it. Adults, however, must learn that if a spontaneous act will interfere with gaining more meaningful and lasting gratification over the long haul, it should be restrained.

Suppose I encounter a beautiful and sexually desirable woman crossing the street. If, instead of driving on when the traffic light changes, I race out of the car and drag her off, the immediate gratification may be delightful, but the long-range deprivation of prison life will be crippling. The price is too high.

Learning to channel immediate desire through socially acceptable forms of behavior enables us to retain the privileges of membership in the society, particularly the right to love.

There is residual narcissism in all of us. How much varies with each individual because it is determined by biological predisposition and life experiences. Thus the ability to love is relative at best.

Biological predisposition is directly transmitted from our parents through inherited traits and familial tendencies. We reflect the genetic makeup of our parents. However, environmental factors such as the degree of childhood deprivation or gratification also influence our capacity for loving. Both biological and environmental factors are critically determined by the nature of one's family.

The extent to which we move away from the dependent role assigned to us within our family determines our potential for mature love. The very fact of children's dependency forces them into more narcissistic love relationships. Their weaknesses force them to look out only for themselves, and so they form attachments to others solely in order to fulfill their own needs.

Children frequently tell mothers and fathers how much they love them. This is an announcement of affection that should always be acknowledged by parents. However, it is important—maybe crucial—to help children understand that these loving feelings reflect, to a large degree, the extent to which parents provide comfort and security. We can truly love our parents only if we grow to a position of independence in which

30

we no longer need them to give definition to our lives. Only when we no longer have a great need for the nurturing support of our parents will we be able to choose to love them as individuals in their own right—not because we were born their children, but because we genuinely like them as human beings.

Such an accomplishment makes it possible to enter into a similar loving relationship with other human beings, a relationship based primarily on choice rather than on a need to be nurtured.

4 /

The Family Faces Obsolescence

An infant who is raised without a stable, single mother figure is irreversibly crippled in terms of his potential for loving. This syndrome, called "institutionalism," was observed in a study of the effect of excessive maternal deprivation among foundlings.

In hospital nursing centers and foundling homes, nursing care is provided in eight-hour shifts. A given infant is exposed to at least three—probably more—different mothering figures during the course of each day. This situation is further complicated by the rotation of working schedules to cover holidays and weekends. Studies of children raised in such institutions from birth reveal that the multitude of maternal figures serves to undermine the effective transition of a child from a narcissistic animal to a caring human being. Research indicates that in the absence of a more constant nurturing source for about the first two years of life, the child's ability to love another is severely hindered. The dependency ties that would make possible his social development as a caring person have not been established.

Poverty also compromises a child's opportunity to obtain adequate nurturing. When both parents are forced to leave the home in order to support the household, by accepting work any place and any time they can find it, the child must be cared for by others who are frequently only marginally competent. More often than not, they are too old or too physically handicapped to obtain suitable employment. The collective demands of children ranging in age from infancy through adolescence are so great that only minimal gratification is available on an individual basis. As in the case of institutionalized infants, children in this situation are inadequately mothered. They are left to grow like weeds, propelled exclusively by their own initiative.

Denied the restraining influence of dependency, these children maintain their primarily narcissistic nature throughout life. They are never adequately inducted into society because they will not accept the inherent restraints required by the social structure. Thus, excessive deprivation causes them to forfeit social membership and even to attempt to undermine all restrictive forces. They are left at war with society.

Poverty is not the only source of maternal deprivation. Accidental tragedies and natural disasters can suddenly terminate the existence of caring parents, abruptly cutting off the availability of adequate dependent gratification. The aerial bombardments during World War II resulted in a large number of European children suddenly and tragically deprived of parents. Studies of these children revealed a critical loss of ability to love in many cases. The extent to which each of them was damaged was relative to the child's age at the time his parents were killed and to the duration of his orphaned state. Not surprisingly, the younger the child and the longer the orphaned period, the more severe the loss.

An interesting and unexpected finding involved those children fortunate enough to have a surviving older sibling who could act as a maternal substitute. Such sibling support seemed to immunize the younger child from a serious loss of his capacity to love. This pattern is not dissimilar from the behavior noted in children's reactions to divorce. In the case of an ineffective dissolution of a marriage, where irreparable damage is done to any subsequent family life, children turn to siblings for support.

It is important to note that the very wealthy may also deprive their children of parental dependency. Preoccupied by their own quest for pleasure, the affluent often delegate child rearing to nurses and governesses. Left without a constant and effective nursing person, the infants of the wealthy, like those of the poor, can be deprived of adequate mothering.

Material deprivation is not a critical factor in maintaining a child's potential to grow into a loving person. The essential quality is mothering. Without it, development of the state of dependency between parent and child that will promote the shift from narcissism to caring is impossible.

The critical significance of early mothering in developing the capacity for caring behavior is evident in lower animals as well. It has been shown that puppies separated from their mothers without an appropriate period of weaning make poor pets. The deprivation of adequate maternal nurturing undermines the puppy's potential for affectionate attachments to people or other animals.

The cultivation by parents of the benevolent dependency of their child is absolutely essential in order to motivate him to deny his own narcissism. It is the only means by which he can learn to need another human being.

The dependent ties fostered by nurturing are formed within the context of a family, and its ultimate value is directly related to the duration of the dependent relationships that are established. The difference between good and bad family functioning lies in the

extent to which this dependency is excessively cultivated as a compromising force. In the more effective
family there is a willingness to support the dependent
relationship, but not to the extent that it cripples
the growing child's potential for future pleasure. In the
less effective family, socialization is achieved at the
price of permanently scarring the potential of an individual to attain the stature of an independent adult.

As loving adults, all of us suffer in varying degrees
from having retained some dependent ties with our
parents. The very ties that initially make possible our
ability to care ultimately interfere with the capacity
they serve to form—our ability to love others.

By definition, dependency does not permit us to
assert ourselves through independent choice. This
factor influences every area of our lives.

In terms of sexual functioning, the more dependent
are less able to express themselves in intimate, spontaneous interaction. They are driven to the mechanics
of performance in order to gain reassurance during
lovemaking. In terms of work, dependency is reflected
as an exaggerated need for security, such as status and
money, that is usually pursued at the expense of personal self-expression. For the excessively dependent,
money becomes mother's milk. These people are driven
to collect money compulsively as a means of protecting
themselves from an endless variety of insecure feelings.

It is the dependent needs of parents that cultivate
dependency to an excess in their children. These parents are unable to permit their children to become
individuals with identities of their own and are driven
to force them into exaggerated positions of attachment.
They strive to promote a state of perpetual dependency, which guarantees the lifelong presence of children
within the family orbit and protects the parents from
the painful feelings of separation.

The excessively gratifying parent binds his children
to him by seducing them with a host of dependent

services. He provides his child with unearned privileges that cheat the child of the opportunity to earn his own self-esteem. Such a parent may deceive himself into believing he does this for the sake of the child. In fact, it is done so that he can maintain control over the child.

The mother who is always there whenever the child needs her makes it unnecessary for the child to be there for himself. She soon becomes "Mother Courage" in the child's mind, a symbol whose presence ensures his sense of security. Her existence guarantees his feeling of well-being. This serves to give her a sense of purpose in life, but at the expense of her child's, whose feelings of worth become subordinated to hers.

Through excessive use of nurturing devices, the mother creates a great indebtedness to her on the part of a child, which provides her with an effective means for indoctrinating guilt.

Through guilt, parents can ensure a child's attachment to them. They can mask the distorted use of their children as a means of protecting themselves from loneliness. Guilt serves to reinforce the dependency that limits the extent to which a child can emerge as a free, autonomous individual. In this fashion, it further anchors each child to the family.

Utilizing well-cultivated feelings of indebtedness due him from a child, a parent can provoke guilt at will. Guilt is the parents' means of establishing a line of instant credit available on demand. The more the parent assumes the child's responsibilities, the more the child is constantly conditioned by reminders of all the things the parent has done for him—providing excessive availability of money, protection from competitive failure, and a broad freedom from responsibility. Painful feelings of shame and worthlessness plague the child whenever he disappoints the parent. The need to obtain parental approval in order to avoid the painful impact of guilt compromises a child's ability to act in terms of independent choices and provides the parent with a unique means for manipulating his behavior.

An elaborate system of rights and wrongs is created in the mind of the growing child that reflects his need for their approval. It grows out of the value system of his parents and is then reinforced by judgments of good versus bad externally imposed on his behavior by parental surrogates—teachers, police officers, and clergymen.

In a highly structured form, such value judgments become institutionalized through the fabric of organized religion. Religion provides a set of moral judgments that serve to impose further external restraints. It constitutes one of the means by which man strives to control himself from himself by altering his basic narcissistic state. Generally, religion leads us to believe that our innate biological drives are evil. We are taught to fear and deny them. Religion is a system through which the family, as the first society, is incorporated into the institutions that support the broader society.

In some ways it is more difficult to be an effective parent when one is a have than when one is a have-not. In have-not families the child is forced to develop his own ability to provide for himself by the absence of such means within the family. It becomes necessary for the child to broaden his own competitive skills and realize more of his potential. In the case of less privileged families, requiring the child to operate in a self-supporting fashion takes no special strengths because the very absence of means makes no other alternative possible.

In the case of a have parent, however, his ability to provide the means for supporting his child makes it necessary to operate from a posture of choice. When one can easily make material supplies available, the temptation to earn affection and control over the child through bribery is very great. The parent can present himself as a uniquely benevolent person while at the same time addicting the child to an irreversible attachment to him. The child, in turn, seeks to live up to the parent's desires and ambitions in order to maintain the materials and services he can no longer do without.

It requires strength for privileged parents to relinquish such a manipulative option. They must be willing to defer the immediate gratification derived from seductive nurturing in order to enhance the autonomy and independence of the youngster. This is possible only when the parents are committed to freeing their child and only to the extent that they are not dependent on the child to fulfill their own lives. Parents must be willing to permit the child to separate from them.

In the past decade the concept of "togetherness" has become a social slogan. "The family that stays together" is seen as a healthy unit tied by affection. This need not be the case at all. If families remain together too long, they, like dead fish, also begin to smell.

All too often families stay together because they are bound by deeply rooted dependency. There is no exit; no one is free enough to leave.

Members of the same family may remain physically close to one another because they can't trust themselves to make it on their own. They camouflage their weakness with a façade of closeness born of independent choice. In reality, they use the veneer of caring to create a climate of mutual indebtedness so that each will be unable to leave the other. The combination of dependency and manipulative guilt guarantees survival for all.

Each member of such a family group often blames the other in rationalizing his own inability to leave— "I don't stay for myself, but because she needs me and I can't let her down." In reality, one plays the game only if one wants to, staying out of choice, not necessity. It is just easier to deny one's own weakness and ascribe one's actions to the needs and fears of others.

Indefinite imprisonment within the confines of the family invariably gives rise to hostility. Indeed, hostility is often the cement that binds the family together.

Suffocating togetherness born of dependency will breed either submission and compliance or rebellion. These behavioral forms merely represent opposite sides of the same coin. Both are the result of overreaction to a controlling figure.

The forty-year-old successful bachelor who goes to the psychiatrist because he still cannot act without his mother's approval is not much further along when, after a brief period of therapy, he announces that he "threw the old bitch out and doesn't care what she thinks any more." Real growth would be reflected in his ability to accept his mother for what she is and to make his own personal choices. He need neither treat her royally nor abuse her cruelly. He need only separate from her emotionally.

Togetherness can be a positive and beautiful experience when it is derived from choice. Choosing to be together after attaining independence is very different from a sticky adhesion between people born out of a fear of being alone. The distinction can be made only by determining the freedom of each member to act out of personal choice. However, to be able to act in this fashion, one must first be able to separate and live independently. Only when one does not need to live together can he choose to live together.

Some families appear to function as integrated units in almost all manner of undertakings. At parties they seem to enjoy one another, preferring one another's company to that of others. Most striking is their commitment to work collectively at resolving all sorts of personal crises in the lives of each individual member.

Interestingly enough, such families appear to experience a great number of crises; this is not by chance alone. Examination of the dynamics of the family usually reveals that the apparent increase in problems is a direct outgrowth of the need of the family to have some point of focus on which to center their attention. This need provides a recurrent process that helps maintain a corrupting togetherness. When members of the family begin to drift apart, a crisis surfaces and offers the ideal opportunity to reunite. It functions as a signal to rally and recommit themselves to the ties that bind the family members together.

Such a family-crisis syndrome is based on an unwritten pledge by all members to intrude upon the right of one another to work out their own choices separately. It serves to block any sense of autonomy by individual members. As is the case with society in general, it is usually the most insecure in the family who are the most active in advocating family union. The weak have the most to gain. Consequently, they are the most adroit at playing the role of the dedicated champions of the family.

The need of the weak to maintain themselves through the family often masquerades as benevolence. They never forget a birthday and are always the first to volunteer to undertake peacemaking missions or to provide the excuse—and the facility—for a family gathering, such as birthdays, marriages, births, and even deaths.

Beneath the mask of benevolence the dependent members of a family thrive on the misfortunes of others. This situation gives them a chance to be needed and to build up a reservoir of obligations upon which they can draw in the future.

It all becomes a chain of dependent events. The unfulfilled parents feed off their young by indulging them. The young, in turn, become so dependent on their parents that their capacity for loving others is compromised because of the fears and the guilt estab-

41

lished by parental obligation. Consequently, their own marriages are destined to be relatively unfulfilled and they, too, are subsequently driven to feed off their children.

The only way to break such a chain of events is for a given child to reach a state of independence. This would permit him to challenge the values of his parents. In order to undertake such a challenge, he must first be able to provide for himself and thereby resolve his need for parental nurturing. To establish an identity of his own, he must be able to pay the price. He must be able to negate the seductive gratifications provided by his parents and to attain personal esteem through competitive, self-sustaining efforts.

If he is capable of accomplishing this, he will have the capacity to enter into a loving relationship with another person. But even if he succeeds in consummating a loving relationship, he is still not home free. He will have to work constantly to maintain such a relationship.

All loving relationships are always in jeopardy. To care deeply about someone other than one's self is an unnatural human act. The natural human inclination is to care only about one's self. So it requires constant effort to sustain a loving posture in the face of the relentless pressure of narcissism.

There is no more complex problem that faces loving partners in their common commitment to protect and sustain their love for each other than the issue of sharing their lives with their own children.

All too often children are born out of moments of narcissistic excitement during passionate lovemaking when, consciously or unconsciously, partners seek a child as a creative extension of their love. In such instances the child is viewed as a living representation of the deep feeling they share for each other. But love cannot easily be extended to include a third party.

The practical reality of having a child is far more complicated than the expression of a romantic fantasy. Even at their best, children are great intrusions into a loving relationship between two adults. While children function to supplement the dimensions of the adults' lives, they also extract a great price by inevitably constricting the romantic dimensions of a marriage. It is difficult to sit by a fire sipping wine and eating cheese when a baby is crying. It is difficult—almost impossible —to make love spontaneously when surrounded by the presence of others. Children force parents to relegate their intimacy to the privacy of the bedroom and only at selected times. As the family grows, parental love must increasingly be scheduled to fit into those few fleeting moments when privacy is permitted.

These prices extracted by the presence of children are not meant to dissuade people from planning a family. They are intended to demonstrate the impact of the responsibility for children on the lives of the parents. Such a decision deserves the most careful consideration and must be precisely weighed against the balance of the loving relationship between husband and wife.

Unfortunately, there is less room in the relationship for a child if two adults are truly, deeply, in love. Commitments to each other that lovers must maintain in order to go on loving compromise both their willingness and their capacity to share themselves with children. Their energies and interests are diluted by their involvement with each other.

The painful reality of life is such that the intrusive presence of an innocent child can destroy the romance between husband and wife. They can continue to love each other but may not be able to sustain the feeling of being in love with each other.

Consider the unfortunate example of the woman who is deeply in love with her husband and seeks to bear a child for him as an expression of her love. The pregnancy would fulfill her sense of femininity and thereby enable her to give to him an aspect of herself that she could never share before. The husband lovingly accepts this gift from his wife, and both eagerly await the arrival of the "love child."

The child is born of the best intentions, but its arrival sets in motion an unexpected chain of events. The normal demands of the infant begin to compete with the loving needs of the parents for time and attention. In particular, the nurturing requirements placed on the mother by the baby set up a natural rivalry between the child and his father for her attention. Both parents are forced to divert interest from each other to the child. This introduces a new dimension into the marriage. Their relationship is changed. What started out as an expression of caring between two people ends up as a redirection of some of their energies from each other to a newly arrived third party. And he is there to stay.

When the dimensions of loving between the parents are diluted, the household shifts to a more child-centered home. Parents become more involved with their children and the attainment of social success than with each other. In such instances, the children grow up in the framework of a distorted prototype of love between men and women. In the mind of the child, loving becomes subordinated to parental responsibility and family achievements.

The child-centered home is highly destructive to children. Such a concept is simply another misguided contribution of oversimplified, homespun psychology. Like "togetherness," it has emerged as a positive slogan popularized by the media. It is difficult to read a newspaper or a magazine, watch television, or listen to the radio without being exposed to some generalized commentary about human psychology. One of the more destructive ideas submitted through the media to parents is the glorification of the role of children in the family. The home should not revolve around children. It should be anchored in the loving commitment between the parents, whose relationship should provide the prototype for meaningful life to children. The child should find himself subordinated to his parents' love for each other. Indeed, his awareness of his subordination ultimately motivates him to leave the home in search of a similar relationship for himself.

A child-centered home increases the resistance of children to assume a competitive adult role in society. Their elevated sense of importance drives them to cling to the protective comforts of their household. They quickly learn that the outside world will not grant them the special rank of "prince" or "princess" they have been given in their own home. The sense of specialness that grows out of the child-centered environment distorts a child's image of himself by increasing his narcissism.

Parents who themselves are not free and fulfilled through loving must feed off their children. They seduce the child into postures of exaggerated dependency in order to ensure his continued presence. This causes fear and insecurity in the child and drives him into a life style in which he is less capable of friendship and compassion. He is too filled with envy by virtue of his own dependent limitations coupled with narcissistic ambitions. He compensates by passing judgments on others. He seeks to diminish them as they threaten him by attaining levels of success he cannot achieve. He joins the growing band of elitist groups who put others down to protect themselves from their own narcissistic weaknesses.

In expressing love toward others, one permits them to be themselves. It is the greatest gift one can give to another human being. Therefore, we should constantly seek to provide those we love with opportunities to enable them to establish and maintain their own identity.

It follows that in the process of socialization, loving parents would direct their efforts at freeing the child they had previously captured. They would permit and encourage him to make his own choices as often as possible. They would train him to pay his own prices whenever possible.

The more we do for our children, the less they can do for themselves. The less they do for themselves, the more we have cheated them of the opportunity to earn self-esteem. For self-esteem can only be earned; it cannot be given.

Many parents deceive themselves into believing that they can give a child a real sense of self-worth. They seek to accomplish this by constantly reassuring him that he is a talented individual of special value. They help him deny and rationalize his limitations. Concurrently, they exaggerate his abilities.

Take the example of the first-grade child who brings home from school a drawing that he made in class. Already aware that his was one of the worst, he shows the picture to his parents. The parents, however, tell him that they like the painting and encourage him to believe that he may even have some artistic talent. This was not their honest judgment, but it reflected their efforts to help him build up his self-confidence.

Unfortunately, the child knows better. He is left with a feeling that his parents are lying to him or that they are totally incapable of effectively evaluating his work relative to that of other children on his grade level.

Not only have the parents failed to increase the child's sense of self-esteem; they have also succeeded in eroding some of his confidence in them. It would be far better if they were able to point out affectionately that whatever his talents may prove to be, art doesn't seem to be one of them. This kind of truthful exchange reveals to the child that his parents can accept him for what he is. It makes it unnecessary for him to pretend to be more than he is in order to play the "power-of-positive-thinking game" with his parents. Telling a child how wonderful he is isn't enough. He must believe it himself. He will not believe it merely because his parents have said so. He will believe it when he has earned his own respect by virtue of his own actions.

The more a child is permitted to successfully assume responsibility for himself, the greater is his self-esteem. As his self-esteem grows, it permits the child to accept himself more fully. In accepting himself, he is able to acknowledge his limitations as well as his abilities.

At the very instant of our birth, our biological makeup establishes some of our limitations. We enter the world with innate differences in our biological potential. There will be differences in our intellectual endowments that go beyond the possibility of alteration through education; some of us will be brighter than others. There are differences in our physical appearance. Some of us will be muscular and tall, others less muscular and short. Some of us will be seen as attractive and others as unattractive. There are inborn differences in the extent to which we will be capable of response to external stimuli. When exposed to apparently similar circumstances, some of us will perceive some forms of sensory stimulation that others will not.

Our biological makeup provides an inborn core of constitutional endowments that together with experiences, will constitute our being throughout our lives. It is capable of change only within certain limits. No man can change the basic nature of his biology. He can, however, grow to realize the most of what it has to offer. One can never grow to be more than he is innately capable of being; one is always less, however, when he is unwilling to be himself.

It is, of course, an insult to our sense of omnipotence as parents that we are unable to absolutely regulate the development of our children. Consequently, many parents choose to reject such an intrusion into their parental sense of omnipotence and instead elect to view their child as someone who enters the world as a "blank screen," with no fixed qualities except the potential to reflect the experiences to which he is exposed. This makes it possible for them to think of themselves as having the power to make of a child the kind of person they want him to be. They see themselves as being able to mold his ultimate character structure.

Such a view provides parents with an opportunity to prove their worth through the accomplishments of their offspring. It also allows them to compete with other parents who seek to measure themselves by the achievements of their children. So the parents paste the sticker of the college their child attends on the window of their car, displaying it like a merit badge, particularly if it identifies one of the more prestigious schools in the country.

For anyone who wants to mold things, however, clay is better than people. Abraham Lincoln may have wanted us to believe that all men are created equal, but this is unfortunately not true. Beginning with our first breath, each of us is a unique animal with capacities different from anyone else.

A parent should understand the biological boundaries of his child's makeup. Each child should be helped to grow within the limits of his own unique structure. Parents should not mislead him into pursuing a life style that seeks to go beyond his biological equipment.

Regretfully, this has too often not been the case. There has been a progressive increase in the role assumed by parents in American society. This has been accompanied by the elaboration of the role of the family in our lives. The family has been extended far beyond its initial social purpose. Today it no longer functions primarily as the site for developing a tran-

sient period of dependency in order to convert narcissistic children to caring people. The dependent ties
established between parent and child are no longer
merely a means to an end, but have grown to become
ends in and of themselves.

This is best reflected in the extent to which the
period of adolescence has become prolonged in our
society. Adolescence is a developmental stage artificially set up by man during which the responsibilities
of adulthood are deferred. It is designed to resist the
biological reality that at puberty the child is capable
of reproduction and of providing his own food and
shelter. It serves to postpone moving to a posture of
taking care of others in favor of retaining the posture
of being taken care of.

The more complex the society, the longer the post-
ponement; more time is invested as an apprentice to
adulthood. In primitive societies, for example, there is
no significant period of adolescence. Puberty rites signify immediate stature as a functioning adult member
of the community. The boy proves his merit as a hunter
and becomes a man.

In our society the elaboration of the adolescent
period has presently reached a new peak. Many of our
men and women remain junior members of society and
wards of their families through the first thirty years of
their lives. And that period is continuing to lengthen.
For some, it is approaching the fourth decade of life.

Such a sustained period of nurturing intrudes into
the natural flow of biological development. We have
created a period of dependency extending beyond any
previously known to man. Young people today spend
the most vital and productive years of their lives as
trainees rather than as active participants in society.

Beyond the initial socialization of the child, the
family serves no special purpose. It was intended as a
temporary shelter in which the child is transformed
from a narcissistic individual to a socially oriented

human being. As little time as is necessary should be devoted to the accomplishment of this social transition. As soon after the early period of seductive parental protection as possible, the child's dependency should be discouraged. Instead, he must be given sufficient time to recapture the greater part of his lost autonomy.

We are all familiar with the mother who has a need to bind all the members of her family to her. She seeks to establish the family as an oasis where each child can forever take shelter from any outside pressures that he encounters in life. The parent discourages separation and rewards attachment with physical protection and material gifts. The family becomes a club in which membership guarantees survival.

In exchange, she demands loyalty; a demand that is structured in terms of expressions of parental respect and responsibility to all the other members of the family. She seeks to persuade her children that trust can exist only among family members. All outsiders by definition are suspect.

Those who gain entry into the family circle by means other than that of birthright are relegated to the role of second-rate citizens. There are no exceptions, not even for the spouses introduced to the family through the marriages of the children. The commitment is clearly to the mother's own bloodline. It is the only guarantee of full membership.

Such family configuration sustains dependent states indefinitely. Soon it sets up a circle of events that constantly recycles itself. The dependent child emerges as the dependent parent of the next generation. He repeats the process of parental seduction because he continues to need the support of the family structure for himself. He binds his children to the family just as he was bound before them. In time, the dependent attachments are extended from the parents to the family as an institution in and of itself.

Growing up in such a household is not designed to lead to independent adult life. Instead, it is a place where adolescence lasts forever, because no one is encouraged to leave and stand alone.

How does one escape from such a family? How does one break the self-perpetuating chain of events?

The dependent child of today is destined to become the dependent parent of tomorrow. Consciously or unconsciously, he usually seeks a marital partner who is as dependent as he is, because it is too risky to attempt a loving relationship with an independent, autonomous person who probably would not settle for nurturing him. She would demand a level of independence from him that he could not sustain.

His dependency, therefore, leads him to establish a compromised state of loving in his marriage. He turns to his family to fill the void. He seeks from them dependent and narcissistic gratifications to compensate for his inability to love more deeply.

It is clear that to break the pattern, the child must have a capacity to love that is greater than his parents'. This, in turn, would lead him to be a more loving parent. Only loving parents can succeed in restricting the influence of the family in modern life. Only loving parents can teach their child not to permit himself to be strangled by dependent helplessness. Only loving parents can encourage their child to find his own way before his dependency reaches a point of no return.

In the United States we are experiencing a simultaneous increase in both poverty and affluence, a period of economic expansion that is characterized by the growth of the middle class. The home in the suburbs and the two-car garage have become a relatively common way of life. However, the good fortune of the middle class has not been accompanied by an increase in the resources of the poor. Instead, what has developed is the formation of a widening gap between the middle and lower classes. Economists report that for the first time in our history the lower class is relatively fixed. For these people it is increasingly difficult to gain upward mobility, for it is now harder than ever before to move from rags to riches.

Throughout the country, inner cities are characterized by growing poverty. Many of our urban centers are on the verge of bankruptcy. There is a breakdown in available social services. Our public-school facilities are crowded and the quality of education is seriously compromised. The affluence represented in the development of comfortable suburban communities is not reflected in the core of our urban centers.

As our society is constituted today, both excessive deprivation and excessive gratification are more prevalent than ever before—and both encourage the persistence of narcissism.

Deprivation is more than an abstract economic reality; it is a condition to which the poor are constantly exposed. Through the pervasiveness of the media, the discrepancy between the poor and the always acquiring middle class is constantly visible. This sets off feelings of deprivation that lead to resentment and rage. Parents' hostility is transmitted to their children, who are made to feel there is no escape from their fate. Their sense of helplessness is exaggerated and exacerbated. Whatever capacity for loving they might have is diluted in narcissistic rage.

The United States today is experiencing a contemporary form of feudalism. As individual members of the middle class accumulate more and more wealth, inheritance becomes a determining factor in the expectations of a rapidly growing number of our young.

We have developed our own privileged society. More and more children are excessively rewarded with protective services and material goods as a consequence of birthright rather than for their accomplishments in an openly competitive society. We educate them to live in a world of specialness.

When I first began to practice psychiatry, I was frequently consulted by parents who were seeking an evaluation of the development of their children. They were anxious about the normalcy of their young. They came to be reassured that things were progressing within normal limits.

At that time, if, on the basis of my findings, I reported to parents that they had "a nice, normal, average youngster," they were relieved and delighted.

Today when I describe a child as "average," the parents leave my office depressed. The new yardstick of appropriate behavior insists upon certain qualities of specialness. The name of that game is narcissism.

5 /

Adolescence:
The Point of No Return

Adolescence is a time of maximum resistance to further growth. It is a time characterized by the teenager's ingenious efforts to maintain the privileges of childhood while at the same time demanding the rights of adulthood. It is a point beyond which most human beings do not pass emotionally.

By the time we are teenagers we have been intensely trained to view life as an experience surrounded by parental support. We have learned to be dependent on another object, and this exaggerates the risks of autonomous, independent behavior. Since independence is not a critical necessity prior to adolescence, the earlier requirements for sustained growth were never as threatening. Before the adolescent period the natural pattern of growth did not face serious opposition to further progression. Adolescence, however, by virtue of the fears inherent in contemplating separation from parents, precipitates a resistance to growth that persists throughout our lives. This is a force that must be overcome in order to attain the sense of identity that marks adult integrity.

We, as parents, do not maliciously seek to curtail the potentials of growth in our children. Indeed, we would consciously like their lives to be as fulfilled as possible. However, our behavior is not exclusively a result of our conscious, rational capacities, but reflects the irrational influences that make us human as well. Only by facing our emotional limitations can we parents learn to deal with the challenges brought on by living with adolescents.

The generation gap has never been more clearly defined than it is today. Adults in our society find themselves overwhelmed by trying to understand this sharply different adolescent generation, one whose values, behavior, and appearance are dramatically different from its elders. Adolescents use drugs in unprecedented amounts. They dress in a fashion that challenges adults. They attack the lovelessness existing in the world. They decry violence and war. They demand greater sexual freedom. They loudly protest social injustice. They have effected educational reforms. They have attacked the materialism and goals of the established community to the point where their rebelliousness sometimes borders on anarchy.

It is increasingly evident that adolescence is not a joyous and footloose period of life. This transitional stage between childhood and adulthood is characterized by turbulence, uncertainty, and confusion. It is a time of disillusionment, when fantasies of childhood are tested against the realities of competitive survival as an adult. It is a time so packed with conflict that the task of resolution is often overwhelming.

Throughout the history of this country, the teenager has always been associated with rebellion, owing to the fact that adolescence is a transient period of exaggerated idealism.

Some have argued that this generation of adolescents is not significantly different from those that preceded it. They take the position that teenagers always had unique fashions of dress and speech. They compare the rock music of today to the swing of the forties, and the present fashions to the zoot suit. They lull themselves into a false sense of security in the hope that "it will all pass—just as it always has."

The fact is that the adolescent community today is different from any other we have ever known. It reflects a change in the character structure of Americans. Adolescents are an extension of our society's inability to handle its success effectively. As did all societies in the past, we are finding it nearly impossible to contain the corrosive impact of great affluence. This adolescent generation is forcing us to deal with the question of whether or not we are capable of managing the insidious effects of our accumulation of political and economic power.

Traditionally, adolescence is looked upon as the time when the teenager directs his efforts toward the pursuit of independence. Our sophisticated society no longer utilizes simple puberty rites to define this coming of age. In its place we have established a long period of containment during which the adolescent works to achieve his own philosophy of life and to extricate himself from the clutches of his parents. In accomplishing this, he intermittently rebels against all forms of established authority, which he views as an extension of parental restraint. His overriding purpose is to find a loving relationship outside the confines of his home. He is faced with the need to acquire sufficient financial resources of his own so that he can entertain thoughts of marriage. He approaches the posture of an adult in the social community, but such a posture requires a major shift from the position of being taken care of to one of taking care of others.

Overwhelming self-doubt invariably accompanies adolescence. It is an inevitable outcome of the intense struggle that preoccupies this stage of development, a totally consuming conflict between the adolescent's desire to remain dependent and his wish to become independent. He can opt to passively acknowledge the physical attributes of aging but remain psychologically fixed on childlike quests for security. Without further emotional growth on his part, he may marry, have children, and raise them to the point where they are capable of producing their own offspring. On the other hand, he can elect to sever the parental ties that have bound him and stand on his own. The reality is that most of today's teenagers expend their efforts at preserving their right to be taken care of as children.

No total resolution is possible in the adolescent's struggle for autonomy. There is no such thing as total independence, given the human condition.

In navigating his way through this highly volatile period, the teenager constantly competes with the real and imagined accomplishments of those who are his adolescent peers. This competitive preoccupation is painful. The need to rank oneself is relentless. It is a reflection of his difficulty in accepting his own physical, emotional, and social limitations.

His overriding fear is that if he gives up his dependent supports, he will vanish into the hordes of the anonymous and undistinguished. He wants to establish an identity of his own. He needs to forgo the identity given to him by his parents, but in the agonizing time-warp of adolescence there is yet no identity of his own. There is only the opportunity to struggle to find one. The moment of truth comes when he either steps out or stays.

On the way to that moment of truth the adolescent employs the techniques of mastery to protect himself from fears of mediocrity. At first he directs his attention to those areas of his life where he can acquire control by practice. This is useful in dealing with the more rational aspects of behavior, because it permits high levels of performance in such areas as academic studies and mechanical or athletic skills.

Mastery, however, is ineffective in dealing with the

irrational core of life. The capacity for caring cannot be practiced or exercised in a mechanical fashion. It grows out of our freedom to permit expression of our feelings. It requires a willingness to be vulnerable. It cannot be mastered—not even by adolescents who want to be invulnerable.

This is dramatically evident in the examination of the sexual behavior of adolescents. The teenage years are accompanied by the highest levels of sexual excitement, which preoccupies and consumes a good part of their waking and sleeping lives. Teenagers constantly bombard one another sensually and provoke one another sexually.

Their fears about sexual performance serve to distort the expression of their natural sex drives. Adolescents are uncertain about their capabilities. Consequently, their early sexual behavior is compromised by their need to protect themselves from feelings of inadequacy. That pressure often drowns out the tender, relaxed communication that is the essence of the lovemaking experience.

Sexual compatibility is measured by the extent to which partners can communicate intimately. It is directly related to freedom of self-expression. The adolescent's early sexual experiences, however, are self-serving, initially pursued to gain peer acceptance, to establish himself as being "one of the boys." His commitment is to performance until he is able to develop an adult sexual identity. Many, unfortunately, do not succeed in attaining an adult sexual identity.

Similarly, in social, intellectual, and political pursuits, the adolescent compromises his own identity in order to avoid the risk of group disapproval. This quality of adolescence haunts many of us in our adult lives. We seek to appear independent while conforming to the pressure of peer groups.

Adolescence is a period of difficulty for parents as well as for children. In fact, the issue of independence that dominates adolescence is resisted to some degree by everyone. Since all of us have some residual needs for dependent supports, any expression of independence sets off anxieties in each of us.

The ability to separate is critical for independence, but a group will offer resistance to the separation of its members because separation is a threat to its cohesion and therefore to its survival.

The family is the prototype for all group behavior. There, the demand of one member to separate constitutes a challenge to all the other family members. For the parents, this demand revives the residuals of their own unresolved dependency. Parental dependent needs motivated them to bind their family into an interdependent unit. The extent to which the interdependence entraps the family members reflects the emotional maturity of the parents.

Whenever a child threatens to exceed the level of maturity of his parents, it produces great turbulence within the household. While most parents express the wish for their children to exceed their own accomplishments in life, they nevertheless tend to resist the child when he is about to surpass them.

For example, a mother who has built her entire existence around a dependent relationship with her husband will attempt to thwart her daughter's efforts at developing a career that will permit her to be independent of her own husband. Such a mother rationalizes her need for security in marriage as a statement of intense love and devotion. She may try to persuade her daughter that "men don't like to marry women who are too self-sufficient." She might also insist that a good mother is one who stays at home and makes her family the most important thing in her life. The mother's emotionally charged position camouflages the reality that if children are the most important objects in a parent's life, the parent can never permit separation, for this would leave her without a purpose.

Children represent an extension of the unrealistic feelings of specialness parents require. We are living at a time when one cannot help being impressed by the level of aspiration parents project upon their children. Children are pushed as never before to attain some measure of prominence. This has brought today's adolescent to a psychological point unlike any that has previously existed. Normalcy is no longer adequate; specialness is the uniform of the day.

Specialness is a narcissistic expression of an exaggerated sense of self-adulation. It is often a derivative of success in any form. It is a concept that can be applied individually or collectively.

There are hierarchies of social rank leading to special status in every category of organized groups—from country clubs to religions to nations. For example, we in the United States have all come to think of ourselves as special. Our country is abundant with resources and "we have never lost a war."

Individual narcissism is increased through collective narcissism. By identification with special groups, we become special ourselves. This ranges from the ability to gain admission to Studio 54 to being a graduate of the "right" Ivy League school.

It is all part of a reverberating narcissistic chain of events. Collective narcissism increases individual narcissism and vice versa. It is a little like inflation; once the process gets going, it is hard to stop.

Success in any form, individual or collective, gives vent to insidious priorities that demand privilege. As the world becomes our oyster, we exaggerate our sense of importance in the tide of human affairs. This makes living more perilous. It also progressively deprives us of love.

In our successful society, the tendency to narcissistic growth is further complicated by promiscuous and oversimplified dissemination of psychological ideas.

No better example of the impact of the bombardment of child-rearing advice exists than in the plight of today's adolescent. Experts have attacked his parents everywhere—at PTA meetings, in all forms of mass-media communication, and at cocktail parties—with information to help them raise "the more perfect child." They were told about everything: self-demand feeding schedules; permissive toilet training; child-centered homes; laissez-faire methods of discipline; how to make love, not war; how to protect their civil liberties; how to get rich without working hard; how to get more pleasure out of life, and, most important of all, how to make the most of their specialness.

So we reared a generation of young who sought in the world at large the same sense of specialness and privilege that was enjoyed in the smaller society of the family. To maintain his princely illusions, the teenager restricted his behavior to fit his narcissistic needs. He committed himself to competition only as long as he felt confident of winning. When he anticipated social defeat, he withdrew and protected himself by displacing his failure from himself onto society—it was his teacher, his coach, his mother, his father, the other driver, the other guy, who were to blame. Certainly not himself. He became a willing candidate for rebellious movements. Anything that attacked those external elements that intruded on his need to think of himself as special gained his support.

What a burden we have given our adolescents to bear. The going is never tougher than when our narcissistic shell is pierced and we are forced to give up feelings of specialness. Yet such trauma is unavoidable in any meaningful love relationship. The nature of closeness is such that it accentuates vulnerability. If adolescents cannot tolerate vulnerability because their narcissistic pain is too great, where do they turn for the intimacy of loving?

Today's youth is a generation dedicated to the concept of loving, but they have difficulty practicing what they preach. Their high level of psychological sophistication enables them to identify loving as the center of social life. They invent rituals, write poetry, and sing songs that extol its virtues, yet they find it hard to express in intimate relationships. The narcissistic pain they must endure to maintain a loving commitment is a price that too many of them are unable to pay. The exposure that comes from honest, intimate communication frightens them away. They cop out to protect themselves from the hassles and grief of caring. They live on the sharp edge of a double-edged sword: they believe in love yet are incapable of loving.

Today's adolescents are more depressed than any previous generation's. Their hunger for sustained loving relationships leaves them starving of loneliness. No wonder there has been such an overwhelming increase in suicide; it is now the second leading cause of death among adolescents—and that at a time when the first leading cause is attributable to accidents, a significant number of which are indirect reflections of suicidal behavior.

Why is this generation of adolescents so depressed? Why are they driven to excessive use of drugs to drown out their pain? Why the greater dependency and the artificially induced highs to get through life? Why is there so much anger? Why so much protest? Why so little ability to commit to people, places, philosophies, or purposes? Why the constantly shifting allegiances?

They have more sexual freedom, so they have intercourse more often but make love less often. They have more material possessions yet constantly suffer from want. They have greater opportunities for choice but are less willing to make decisions. What goes on inside them? What is it they see, know, and feel that troubles them so much?

I find today's generation of adolescents to be different from any who have preceded them in three important ways:

1. They are more narcissistic than any prior generation.
2. They are more knowing than any prior generation.
3. They are more dependent than any prior generation.

Their greater narcissism has led them to pursue levels of aspiration so great that it is difficult—if not impossible—to accept mediocrity in any given area. They strive for excellence to the point of distraction. They will not run any race they cannot win. They will defy competition before they will submit. Their standards are oppressive because they leave no margin for error. The high levels they strive for, which reflect what has been imposed on them, make any evaluation that is less than outstanding a condemnation to inevitable failure.

It is not enough to go to college; they must gain admission to the best one. It is not enough to be admired by another, unless that person is one of the most desirable. It is not enough to practice a craft or pursue a profession; they must obtain distinction and visible signs of recognition.

They are not satisfied to stay at the bottom and work their way up. They seek to start their lives where their parents left off and go up from there. None of this is easy to do; most of it is impossible.

Already plagued by their aspirations, they are further burdened by an inability to fool themselves. They are a generation far more knowing and informed than any previous group of young people, and such a level of awareness makes self-deception difficult and serves to increase their sense of conflict. Their knowledge helps to make life fuller, but also more troublesome. Their ability to perceive and to understand requires of them a greater facility at making choices.

When the educational process speeds ahead of the natural rhythm of growth, anxiety is created because of a lack of the skills to perform the learning tasks that are set up. Without the capacity to see, it is ridiculous to teach sight reading. Without the capacity to hear, it is foolhardy to study music appreciation. Without the capacity to walk, it is ludicrous to teach the skills of running. Similarly, without developing the capacity of the adolescent to make choices, it is destructive to bombard young people with the kind of information that leads to an almost endless stream of choices.

The high degree of psychological sophistication that adolescents have today makes it harder for them to deal with themselves and with others. There was a time when a teenager could awaken with a severe headache on the morning of a difficult examination at school, and believe his mother when she told him that his headache was due to an upset stomach. But that can't happen any more. Adolescents know too much about emotional tension and its effects on the body to buy such a flimsy excuse.

Today's adolescent knows when he is behaving to fit the needs of his external image rather than expressing his inner feelings. He knows about his overt contempt for material affluence, but at the same time he is addicted to materialistic excess. He knows his macho façade masks his fears about sexual inadequacy.

The elders in his society don't fool him, either. He is well aware of an adult community that preaches ethical and moral values while misusing their credit cards to avoid income taxes. He is too sophisticated about our national self-centeredness and quests for personal luxuries to accept our pretense at dedication to those two-thirds of the world who are starving to death. He sees through the protest of his elders who attack the use of marijuana while flagrantly abusing themselves through alcoholic consumption.

The adolescent's higher state of knowing makes it harder for him to hide from the truth. Even when he succeeds in denying it consciously, he can't escape from his unconscious. What he knows cannot be turned on and off like a light switch.

His high level of sophistication disillusions him early in his life. It makes finding heroes hard; he knows too much. So he turns instead to anti-heroes. Only disenfranchised young people could permit themselves to rally around Charles Manson. Only a cynical generation with jaundiced convictions about its elders would look to take refuge with Reverends Jim Jones or Moon.

The skepticism of the adolescent about his society's commitment to human ideals extends to his parents, for they symbolize the society. They are the conveyors of social values.

Inherent in the growth of the child is the process of identification with his parents. It is an inevitable part of development. The child who does not respect his parents is angry when he finds himself behaving like them. His identification with them is hostile and leaves him feeling cheated out of idealized figures to model himself after.

One can have loving feelings toward parents and still not respect them as people. One can be appreciative of their loving care and affection and still disapprove of their ethics, personal style, choice of friends, or politics. More and more of our young do not want to grow up to be like their parents. In fact, a common outcry during the course of a quarrel between young lovers is to "stop acting like your mother" (or father, if that happens to be the case). As a rule, such an accusation represents the most violent form of criticism.

The adolescent's dissatisfaction with the social forces around him drives him to want to change them. His sophistication, however, makes it impossible for him to fool himself. All too often he is left with a sense of helplessness because he knows he lacks the means to change what he knows must be changed. Small wonder the young turn for relief from their inability to cope with such reality to flights of fancy and drugs.

Why can't the young be more effective in changing the things in their world that they feel need changing? What makes them unable to support their higher level of knowing with appropriate behavior? Why can't they live up to what they understand? It is their increased dependency, superimposed on their greater narcissism and greater sophistication, that cripples them.

To be able to understand young people today, it is essential to recognize the extent to which they have been made excessively dependent on parental support, because it is that heightened dependency that makes assertive, autonomous behavior so difficult for them. This is particularly crucial to the present generation because it is too knowing to be able to deceive itself about the need for independence in order to be able to love. And the youth today certainly want to be able to love; the messages about love in the poetry and music to which they respond are often brilliant and uniquely insightful. One need search no further than the Beatles, Bob Dylan, Neil Diamond, and Simon and Garfunkel, among the host of writers who have emerged from their ranks, to find illustrations of their profundity.

The actual ability to love, however, is proving to be more and more elusive for the adolescent, because he is thwarted by his inability to overcome the excessive intrusion of the child-centered parents who are constantly hovering around him. His dependency on them blocks him from giving purpose to his own life by achieving his own separate identity.

The ingenuity of parents at maintaining a role in the life of their child can extend adolescent dependency indefinitely. By establishing trust funds that will make it unnecessary for their child to compete in order to earn his own livelihood, they can undermine for an unspecified period his potential to gain self-esteem through supporting himself. By financially underwriting the child's marriage, they can indefinitely postpone his need to accept responsibility for the marital commitment. They can even provide for unborn children and thereby intrude upon the lives of others beyond their own time.

In building their own monuments to immortality, parents need be limited only by their own arrogance, insensitivity, and the size of their estate. It is not uncommon for parents who, above anything else, have prided themselves on being self-made people, to make it impossible for their children to enjoy the same sense of satisfaction.

The ideals that are embraced by the young today require that they renounce many of the practices and standards inherent in their parents' way of life. In this regard, they sometimes confuse protest with dissent. Dissent requires a highly autonomous level of behavior and commitment. It is self-assertive expression accompanied by a willingness to pay the price for dissent. Protest requires only volatility in discharging dissatisfaction and discontent.

The behavior of today's adolescents is characterized by protest rather than by dissent. They attack the very society that they feed upon. Their own conviction of helplessness undermines their ability to commit themselves to programs of social change. They prefer moments of abortive revolution. Their failure to free themselves of the very forces they seek to remove from the existing social structure contributes to a constant sense of self-loathing.

The plight of today's adolescents thus becomes clear. They are a group that believes in loving, when, in fact, their narcissism and dependence make them less able to love. They are a group that attacks the exaggerated need for security at the very same time that they are addicted to the security acquired from being excessively cared for by their parents. They are a society so sophisticated in terms of its own self-awareness that they are unable to deny their own failures to themselves, even when they succeed in hiding them from others. This makes it necessary for them to resort to attacking others as a means of diverting attention from themselves.

Their protest, mistaken for dissent, can be regarded as independent, assertive action, but it is really impotent rage directed at those forces that threaten to overwhelm them. They are particularly vulnerable to feeling overpowered because of their dependent needs. They are not action-oriented, dedicated to change, but an angry, volatile group of people expressing their collective sense of helplessness.

Their ideas are frequently brilliant, and the goals reflecting those ideas are well worth striving to attain. However, their accomplishments provide a naked confession that they cannot live up to what they believe in. Their behavior reveals that they are not an emancipated generation seeking to return to the more fundamental realities. They are a depressed society of young who are imprisoned by their state of knowingness and their inability to act with commitment.

We have made it difficult, if not impossible, for them to act on their choice to become autonomous, loving individuals. We have eroded the potential of their future, and their future is our future.

6 /

Communication:
The Essence of Loving

What is this thing called love? Poets have put it to verse, philosophers have sought to explore its dimensions, and each and every one of us looks for it in his life.

It exists in so many diverse yet interrelated forms: the love between parent and child, between brothers and sisters, between friends, and, at its most intense level, the love shared by lovers.

Are all these forms of love variations on the same theme, or is each one unique? When a parent tells a child, "No one will ever love you as I do," is this so? How does one compare the incredible excitement of a first love affair with the less volatile but more enduring emotional ties of a sustaining relationship? So many of us can look back and wonder what might have been. Is love lost more precious because it is lost, or was it truly destined to be one of those rare experiences? How can we know? How can we measure the potential of a loving relationship? How can we define its intensity, its durability, its total value as the means of maximum pleasure for a social animal?

Do I love someone because I feel excitement whenever she is near? Because we're good together in bed?

Because there is security in her presence? Do I love someone because we've come from similar backgrounds and share similar sociological and ethnic attitudes? Do I love someone because of the stature I gain by being loved by her? Does her beauty and desirability enhance my own?

Loving is none of these things and all of them. It cannot be categorized into separate dimensions. It is a composite of all things.

It is communication, a communication far broader than the written and spoken word. It is the entire range of human sensory behavior, both verbal and nonverbal, through which two people experience each other. We love each other to the extent that we are able to communicate with each other, a communication that extends into all areas of life: social, intellectual, emotional, and physical.

Like all other animal forms, we can experience the world only through our sensory capabilities. To perceive anything, we must first experience some aspect of it. It must be seen, heard, smelled, tasted, touched, or conceived by us in terms of its gravitational influence on our body. There is no other way. Data can reach us only through one of these senses.

Each of us comes into the world with unique sensory configurations. One's individual threshold varies relative to one's ability to taste, smell, touch, see, hear, and feel.

This is obvious when we examine the physically deformed. Those who are almost deaf live in a world nearly devoid of sound. Muffled noises take on a meaning that is different from that experienced by those who can hear. The nearly deaf learn to rely on vibrations in their bones set off by sound. For them, nuances of music, speech, and nature cannot be experienced in the same fashion as they are by those of us who hear normally.

Similarly, those who are born blind cannot collect

a reservoir of visual images to bank in their brains. The sensory images shaped within their minds are inevitably different from those perceived by the seeing. Their images are formed primarily from sound, touch, smell, and taste. To communicate with them, we must find some common area of experience. For example, we can attempt to relate our visual images through touch by using Braille. We can also make use of sound through more explicit verbal descriptions. We turn to other senses in an effort to share the experience of a sight to behold. It is not impossible, but it is different.

To see two deaf people communicating is impressive. Their ability to inject passion into the mechanical structure of sign language reflects their commitment to communication. Their ability to share nuances of feeling through sight and touch is evidence of their search for more intimate communication.

Like the rest of us, the disabled work to reach one another as deeply as possible. In spite of congenital sensory deprivation, the quest for total communication prevails. That quest is the search for love.

Even those of us who come into the world without deformities nevertheless bring with us certain limitations. We hear, see, smell, touch, and taste differently from one another. These differences will shape the quality of our ability to communicate. In turn, our ability to communicate will give definition to our life style. It will mold the dimensions of our character structure.

From the earliest days of our lives some of us are more sensual than others. Some are more responsive to external stimuli, more vulnerable to the constant bombardment of shifting light, sound, touch, taste, and spatial positions. Some are destined for a life of heightened experiences and therefore for a life of greater ferment because of their receptivity.

Others come into the world as relatively less sensual individuals. They are less responsive to external stimuli, less vulnerable to the constant bombardment of shifting light, sound, touch, taste, and spatial positions. They are destined for a life of less intense experiences and, therefore, for a life containing less ferment because of their reduced receptivity.

These configurations, which are set at birth, remain relatively fixed throughout our lives. All of us will fall into one of these two categories. We will be either primarily sensual or less sensual.

Those of us with the primarily sensual configuration make up the character style technically designated by psychiatrists as hysterical personalities. Unfortunately, the word "hysterical" has been distorted to mean excessive emotion, which is judged to be an unstable quality. Nothing could be further from the truth. It merely describes a life style of heightened expressiveness, reflecting a primarily sensual makeup. Because of their constant state of sensory ferment, people with hysterical personalities tend to be less reliable about discipline; consequently they are not given to punctuality, order, and commitment to detail. They deal with life in more holistic and enveloping terms, and because of this, they tend to be more creative. However, their creativity is usually accompanied by impulsiveness. So much goes on inside them that they are always reaching out to express themselves.

They can be sensually promiscuous, touching excessively as they attempt to communicate, needing to taste all the wine, smell all the flowers, feel all the textures, and see all the sights. They possess an insatiability that is fed by their heightened sensuality. Their constant state of flux makes them more exciting but also more frustrating, because they are so tuned in to everything. There is always so much for them to react to, it is hard for them to commit themselves to one thing at a time.

The hysteric relates to life more through feelings than through ideas. He is more prone to exclamation:

74

"It's the greatest! I love it!" He says this so often, its meaning becomes unclear.

The easy accessibility to his feelings makes him attractive, but the fickle nature of his constantly shifting hungers makes him hard to trust. He is lovable, but difficult to love.

Those who are not hysterical characters are less sensual in their configuration. They make up the character style designated by psychiatrists as obsessional personalities. Unfortunately, the word "obsessional" has also taken on a negative connotation. It is too frequently associated with excessive compulsiveness and excessive vulnerability to detail. These individuals are all too often pictured as insensitive to the point where they cannot see the forest because they are so busy counting the trees.

Again, nothing could be further from the truth. The obsessional character comprises a life style of selective expressiveness reflecting a less sensual makeup. Obsessional personalities tend to be people who are more disciplined. Their orderliness and the rhythm of their daily routines are not compromised by constant sensory ferment. They feel less of the time, and therefore fewer feelings are expressed.

They are more exacting about punctuality and reliability. They deal with life in specific and precise terms and are steady and more predictable. Because of these qualities, they tend to be less creative and less exciting. However, they are also less threatened by impulsiveness.

Since not so much is going on inside them, they do not have a heightened need to act out. They are sensually guarded, needing to touch very little or not at all as they attempt to communicate. They don't need to explore new wines or examine new textures. Instead, they are satisfied with what they already know.

The obsessional character relates to life more through ideas than through feelings. He is prone to be critical and exacting in his declarations: "I asked for a two-minute egg, not a three-minute egg." "You're six minutes late."

Similarities in sensual makeup enables us to relate more effectively to others like ourselves. Obsessional people are better able to communicate with other obsessional people. In the same fashion, hysterical people are better able to communicate with other hysterical people.

The irony of human nature is such, however, that we tend to be attracted to those who are not the same as we are. Our inability to accept ourselves directs us to people who are different. By virtue of being dissatisfied with ourselves, we exaggerate the value of attributes we lack when we find them in others.

In the course of my psychiatric practice, for example, I have encountered the hysterical woman who was plagued by the fear that she talked too much. She was constantly on guard to control her tendency to be too expressive. In turn, she found herself regularly attracted to men who were controlled and quiet. She always assumed that strength went with silence. She ultimately married one of these "strong, silent men," only to discover some years later that he was merely silent.

Similarly, the less sensual person delegates excessive values to his more expressive opposite. For him, the more sensual woman is the personification of warmth and affection. She makes it possible for him to experience vicariously the feelings he cannot experience in himself. She provides him with some relief from his greater self-restraint. Her heightened expressiveness represents to him both vitality and a great capacity to love. All too often he discovers it is only vitality.

Our inability to accept ourselves makes loving difficult. It directs us to reject our own life style in favor of another. Consequently, we reach out for people with whom we are less able to communicate. We deceive ourselves about this communicative void through the illusion of romance. Unfortunately, illusion doesn't last long in the face of reality. Such pairings are doomed to mutual loneliness brought on by ineffective communication.

There must be a communicative compatibility between two people to achieve a loving state. While it is true that opposites attract, it is also true that they do not live well together in a loving situation.

For instance, if one partner enjoys a form of music that is utterly alien to the other, they are describing a difference that is not merely one of interest but a rather basic incompatibility in sensory responsiveness. Similarly, if one partner likes films about real people who are part of an intimate love story and the other likes simple action-adventures, the difference may be more real than superficial. Enough of these differences can make intimate communication virtually impossible.

In such incompatible relationships the dominant partner usually attempts to change the less dominant one. In any unhappy marriage one mate is constantly trying to alter the behavior of the other. In an ineffective friendship one individual tries to manipulate the responses of the other. Such futile efforts are doomed to failure. The best one can do is recognize and identify incompatibilities, and respect the differences. Only by accepting a relationship for what it is can one make the best of it. The more a person tries to alter the basic quality of another, the more he will undermine the potential of the relationship as a caring experience.

Since the essence of love is communication, all loving relationships are relative at best. There is no "pure" human experience. The extent to which communicative compatibility exists in a relationship reflects the potential for intimacy and sharing in that relationship. It is central to establishing the intensity of the loving interaction between any two people.

Feeling people do not live full lives if they are married to nonfeeling people. Similarly, relatively nonsensual people can be overwhelmed by the persistent onslaught of a sensual mate. What is perceived by two sensual people as delightful intimacy may well be perceived by a less sensual person as an overpowering and demanding barrage of intrusiveness. Conversely, what is seen by a relatively nonsensuous person as disciplined self-containment may be viewed by a sensual person as isolated, suffocating confinement.

In our society, self-realization can most effectively be achieved and maintained through a loving commitment to another human being. But such a commitment is possible only after an individual has come to know and accept himself; that is essential in order to develop a compatible relationship with another person.

There is no substitute for loving as a self-fulfilling human dimension. Our interests, our work, and our skills are merely supplements to this dimension. Where loving is compromised, these supplementary elements assume a critical significance in neutralizing—at least to some measure—the overwhelming pain of personal loneliness. The individual who cannot love is often driven to power as a means of buffering the emptiness. Our social roles enable some women to achieve such power through excessive mothering. Most men and increasing numbers of women, however, achieve it in their work.

Throughout life we have to be vigilant to protect the integrity of our capacity for loving. Since each of us is constantly bombarded by narcissistic and dependent pressures to compromise, that integrity is always in jeopardy. Each time we sell out a little bit of ourselves, we lose some of our ability to love. Every retreat from independence carries with it some loss of the pleasure of loving.

To love someone is to give that someone the right to be himself or herself. By feeling accepted by another human being, we become freer to be ourselves. It is a reverberating and reinforcing cycle.

The ability to accept ourselves enables us to choose a partner with whom we can communicate. By accepting ourselves we can accept another. The compatible communication, in turn, constantly brings new and added dimensions to the communicative process. By revealing ourselves more fully to that other person, we give them the opportunity to accept us more intimately. The more accepted we feel, the more we can continue to grow in terms of accepting ourselves and others.

We measure love in terms of communicative compatibility. We measure communicative compatibility in terms of the growing freedom to be ourselves. The goal of such freedom is to exist as a real person for at least one other human being during our lifetime. That is loving. That is also the most exquisite form of living.

Loving is the core of adolescent philosophy. The young have grown to acknowledge the conditions that characterize love. They recognize the commitment and courage inherent in exposing one's self to another human being. They acknowledge the total nakedness involved in caring: physical, intellectual, and emotional. They would like to be able to tolerate the anxieties evoked in making themselves completely vulnerable to another. They would like to be able to choose to love.

Unfortunately, we have undermined their capacity to do so by nurturing them excessively within the family unit. We have contributed to their heightened narcissism by eroding their capacity to tolerate the deprivation necessary to acquire self-esteem. We have betrayed their trust by failing to live up to our own commitments. We have exposed them to a generation of elders who say one thing and then do another.

Lovelessness is growing in our society and it is a dangerous quality because the loveless seek power as an alternative. This occurs at a moment in history when modern technology has made possible unprecedented accumulations of power. Power in the hands of the loveless will devastate society.

7 /

Sexuality:
The Intimate Communication

Man has always sought aphrodisiacs. His quest for sexual pleasure has persisted throughout the ages. He has invented rituals, herbal concoctions, and even gods to enhance his efforts.

In our own time entire industries have sprung up related to man's pursuit of heightened sexuality. This goes far beyond an increase in pornography or the plethora of explicit magazines. It is the substance on which much of the advertising industry has been built.

You can sell anything as long as it's sexy. So we put a provocative body in front of a car, an inviting smile by the toothpaste, a seductress by the perfume, a lathered beauty by the bar of soap, and a hirsute football player by the hair spray. That is the name of the game. Advertisers shrewdly understand that they have a built-in market. Man wants as much sex as he can get. Attach it to a product and he'll buy it.

Actually, the only aphrodisiac that has survived throughout the ages—because it is the only one that has ever worked—is communication. When you communicate with someone, you are sexually attracted to that person. It matters not whether it is a sixty-year-old professor or a handsome young athlete, a matronly grandmother or a beauty queen. If someone can reach you and be reached by you, you get turned on.

The advertising industry flourishes because we can't communicate. We are sitting ducks for any artificial substitute that is offered.

Our puritan forefathers understood human vulnerability to sexual programming even better than the advertising industry. They marketed an attitude about sex with incredible success—that sexual behavior as a pleasurable end in itself was evil. They anchored their distorted concept into the fabric of society. It persists even today.

This admonition brought with it the creation of an exaggerated, almost demonic apprehension of any form of sexual expression. The fear of sexuality was so great, it swept along with it all forms of sensuality as well. To protect society against the immorality of making love for sheer pleasure, all forms of intimacy and closeness were rigidly restricted.

Our predecessors constructed the Calvinistic New England ideal: duty, discipline, and responsibility. This contributed to the formation of the idealized image of a sterile person who stringently polices any overt expression of feelings, sexual or otherwise. Man forced himself to fit this mold. This legacy was passed carefully from generation to generation. Its intent is to irrevocably interlock the sensuality inherent in human communication with the sexuality involved in lovemaking. It frowns upon the one and virtually forbids the other.

It is a crippling way of controlling human behavior. It is based on the false assumption that sexuality is such an overwhelming force that it can be controlled only by rigid adherence to total suppression except within the acceptable confines of a marriage, and then only in the intimacy of the bedroom and for the purpose of procreation.

Such an assumption dictates that the only way to

control man's sexuality is to harness it with severe external restraints. By leaving no room for individual choice, it reduces the capacity for sexual pleasure. It relegates man to a position of weakness by implying that the demands of the flesh are beyond his control.

In fact, man's weakness was regarded as so great that it required protection not only from the sexual act but from any temptation that might lead up to it. So all forms of sensuality were buried as well. And with them the potential for any meaningful communication.

In this regard, it is clear that our forefathers were no fools. They were smart enough to recognize that sensual communication would inevitably lead to sexual behavior. They understood that one was an appropriate continuation of the other. So, for their purposes, they wisely shut them both down.

Sexual taboos, of course, extend much farther back into history than our Calvinistic forebears. Almost from the beginning of recorded history man has been careful to police the extent to which he has permitted himself to engage other human beings sensually. As a matter of fact, the only universal quality found in the comparative study of cultures throughout the world has been the consistent presence of a taboo against incest.

The requirement that physical and sensual restraints be established in the relationship between parent and child has been identified in every society known to man. This reflects an awareness of the continuity between sensual communication and sexuality. Even primitive man recognized that the natural flow of the human animal's sexual interests knows no bounds. It exists among members of the same family group, as well as in the society at large.

The family unit, society's cornerstone, could survive only if artificial barriers were placed on human beings living in close contact with one another. This is no less true today than at any other time in man's history. No society can continue to survive unless an effective barrier to incest is maintained. That is the practical function of the incest taboo. It is not an indictment of man, but the recognition of the nature of his innate sexuality.

We are all familiar with both the excitement and the anxiety that one feels when he inadvertently catches a glimpse of his sister's or his mother's naked body. In some instances, the glimpse is not an inadvertent one; sometimes it takes a lot of planning to catch one's sister in an unguarded moment.

We are also aware of both the pride and the embarrassment a son feels when his friends respond to the sexual desirability of his own mother. When they exclaim that "she sure has a great body" or that "she is some dish," he experiences mixed feelings. He is excited by the affirmation of his own sexual attraction and is simultaneously frightened by it.

There is no reason why a mother should not be attracted to her handsome son, or the son to his attractive mother. Such thought is not a shameful human response. Nor is it shameful for the beautiful sister to attract, and be attracted by, a good-looking brother. It reflects a perfectly understandable human quality, albeit one that we must never permit ourselves to act upon.

To maintain social order, the necessity for an incestual taboo is absolutely vital. Each of us must be educated to control such sexual feelings, but not at the price of being forced to believe that these feelings are unnatural.

Each of us must learn to differentiate between the thought and the deed. In thought, we are all polymorphous perverse. There is no sexual act that we have not considered and, in the very process of consideration, been titillated by. Each of us has been a voyeur, an exhibitionist, and a sexual gymnast. Some of us have even thought of ourselves as pornographic film stars.

The human mind is capable of conjuring up all sorts of creative sexual fantasies. Indeed, the publishers of romantic novels live off the boundless permutations and combinations of sexual activities that are conceived by our collective psyches.

But if we excessively indict ourselves for our thoughts, we leave ourselves very little room to navigate our daily lives. Sexual excitement is always going on; it is part of the universal experience of being human, in both homosexual and heterosexual terms. All forms of sensual input set it off, sometimes in what appears to be the most unlikely situations.

Students who remain isolated in their rooms for many hours in order to prepare for an examination have complained to me about their difficulty in restraining intense sexual desires that emerge and distract them from their studies, even though they had no conscious interest in sex when they sat down to study. They were unaware that a period of heightened thought in and of itself can stimulate sexual feelings. The presence of sexual objects, imagined or real, is not always necessary.

Some patients have been embarrassed in reporting to me their interest in making themselves attractive prior to leaving to attend the funeral of a friend or a relative. They were not dressing up only as a tribute of respect to the deceased. They were responding to an awareness that the chapel would be filled with many other men and women. This perception automatically converted the funeral chapel into a place where sexual interests would exist in addition to an assembly of mourners.

The patients felt guilty because they regarded a funeral as an inappropriate time to experience sexuality. Unfortunately, however, sexual interests do not surface only in accordance with feelings about social propriety. We can discipline our behavior to follow the rules of etiquette, but we cannot do the same with our impulses. Nor should we.

Excessively restrained incestual feelings can even result in undermining psychological consequences. It is not uncommon for a husband to have some sexual difficulty in reacting to his wife after she has given birth to a baby. A transition to the role of mother on her part can set off feelings of guilt in him when he approaches her sexually if he has inappropriately displaced incestual feelings from his own mother onto the mother of his own child.

Our puritan heritage leaves us little room for either sensual or sexual interaction. So we dare not touch each other for fear that we would inevitably end up in bed. All forms of communication that require close proximity are restrained. This serves to impose on us a way of life that negates our capacity to make choices. Instead, we are left with the virtues of a system anchored in immoral morality. Much of our behavior does not reflect our own ethical judgment, but only a conformity to limits externally derived and enforced.

If Sigmund Freud contributed anything toward helping man understand himself, it was his thinking about sexuality. He helped us see that our adult sexual desires include—and are an extension of—the sensual events of our childhood. He demonstrated that all forms of human sensory perception contribute ultimately to the makeup of adult sexuality—the sucking of a thumb by an infant, the use of his muscles to move about, the sound of his loved object's voice, and the taste of his favorite food are all precursors of sexual pleasure in the adult. Freud recognized that human sensuality is a critical part of pleasurable sexual expression.

Sensuality, although an inherent part of the sexual complex, is obviously not its total. However, fear of sexuality has been so extreme that it has driven society to attack sensuality as an end in itself.

The witch hunters of Salem murdered the more sensual and perceptive women in the community, branding them as evil. To survive in seventeenth-century Massachusetts, it was necessary to deny sensuality as well as sexuality. The bundling board was used by women to protect themselves from accusations of witchcraft; it blocked sensual and sexual contact.

Hester Prynne, with the scarlet A on her breast, got off easily; others were hanged. But everybody was forced to pay some price. At the very least, one had to deny the sensual component of one's personality. The denial of sensuality, in turn, effectively cut down intimate communication. With intimate communication shut down, sexual behavior as a pleasurable experience was almost impossible.

If man is not free to experience his senses, he isolates himself and seriously limits communication with other human beings. He surrounds himself with an invisible shield that acts as a barrier to restrict the extent to which he permits the outside world to reach him.

Clearly a viable society requires some degree of control over man's sexual behavior. But it does not require that he similarly control his private thoughts or sensibilities. To abandon sensuality in the service of sexuality is like throwing the baby away with the bath water. Nevertheless, we have thrown it away. In fact, we have permitted ourselves to be pushed even further, so that not only is sex considered evil but sensuality as well.

Once sensuality is condemned, the right to pleasure is also condemned. It serves to structure a way of life in which the joys of living are ultimately reduced to the point where the sense of individual fulfillment that is derived from dutiful accomplishment remains as the only relatively guilt-free form of personal pleasure.

Society's need to maintain the viability of the family unit demands adherence to the incest taboo. Man's innate vulnerability to sexual behavior led to the birth of puritanical values to reinforce this taboo, but these puritanical values require the abandonment of sensuality as well as sexuality. Our distorted social prejudice against sensuality makes living complicated for the more sensual person. His very nature constantly drives him to sensual interaction with others. It is the primary means through which he communicates. For him the written word is less satisfactory. Consequently, he lives with a greater sense of communicative isolation within society, and that leads him into frequent states of depression.

It is the sensual person who more often than not seeks psychiatric help. He pays a higher price for living. Greater social adaptation is required of him. On the other hand, he has the greater potential for a full life.

The less sensual among us can more easily accept the loss of sensuality in social living. Their disciplined, ordered life is more compatible with the social requirement of sensual denial. Communication tends to be more rational. Consequently, it is easier for the less sensual person to settle for the written and spoken word. He has an easier time of it, but his life is usually not as full as his sensual counterpart's.

So no one escapes without paying a price. For some it is the difficulty encountered in adjusting to sensual denial. For others it is the less fulfilling nature of their being.

The more sensual, hysterical personality is forever battling with his fear. It operates everywhere. His vulnerability to new sensory input leaves him constantly provoked. If he acts upon the provocation, he faces the risk of censure. If he doesn't act, he lives with the loneliness of communicative isolation. He is faced with a dilemma: React to the exposure and tolerate the pain that it can bring, or play it safe and try to settle for less. Not an easy choice to make, particularly when one constantly hungers to touch, see, hear, smell, and taste.

For the less sensual, obsessional personality, there is not so great a need to constantly monitor new input, because there is less of it. His life is therefore better regulated. Highs and lows are more easily avoided, but the sameness of the middle ground enervates him. Life becomes too regular, too predictable. The monotony of consistency becomes a chore, yet if he reaches out for more, he risks the constancy that is the essence of his life style.

Many of us elect not to pay the price of intimacy. It is too high. Yet the price of living without it is even higher. To exist and yet not to be. To survive and yet not to experience.

With their heightened state of knowing, the youth of today have rejected a life style that suppresses all forms of intimate communication. To make their point, they have exaggerated their sensuality by flagrantly displaying it in their dress, in the intensity of their music, and in their freedom of communication through touch.

Unfortunately, once again their actions are essentially protestation rather than assertive dissension. They cannot commit themselves to their own commandments. Their energies are invested primarily in criticism rather than in sustained action.

Nudity, sexual play, and sensuality are overtly expressed by today's young, but the ease of that expression is an exaggerated defense against exposing their inability to tolerate intimacy. While their knowing has enabled them to perceive the joys of intimate communication, their increased narcissism and dependency make it impossible to attain. The vulnerability of exposure is far too risky for a narcissist. The frustrations that are an inevitable part of closeness are too painful.

In addition, their dependency inhibits the autonomy necessary to sustain the self-expression required by intimacy.

They have diverted attention from their own inability to be more open by creating a great deal of noise about the need to free up society. They employ the tactic of exaggerating the image in order to mask the substance. They flagrantly display their sensuality almost to the point of perversion. But their heightened expressiveness does not function to increase communication. It serves a very different purpose. It is designed to distract attention from their inability to communicate.

They profess commitment to an open society in which "gettin' in touch" is what it's all about. Indeed, they applaud the willingness to touch, smell, hear, and see anybody, any time, any place. Yet their loneliness is even greater than that of their elders.

The young suffer from greater degrees of communicative isolation than the supposedly more inhibited generations before them; not just the isolation evident in their increasing use of drugs but also in their inability to love.

What has their protest about heightened sensuality accomplished? What has their demand for greater freedom to communicate intimately contributed to society? How has their increased sexual activity influenced man's pursuit of sexual pleasure? Are we really freer now? Can we get closer than we ever have before? Is human sexuality more fulfilling? Yes. But not nearly as much as we would like to believe it is.

In the puritan days people suffered from excessive ignorance about human sexuality. And communication between people was so remote that even when sex did take place, it wasn't much fun.

Some things are very different today. Ignorance certainly isn't the problem it used to be. Sexual information is everywhere. Knowledge, curiosity, and experimentation—in all forms—are encouraged. No one can honestly complain that the sexual behavior that is permitted is too little. One can argue that it is still not enough, but it is certainly not too little.

The point is, the attitudes that surround sex have changed a great deal, but the principal quality of our sexual behavior has not. Communication continues to be too remote. We have become master technicians of the sexual act, but we remain unwilling to expose ourselves to the vulnerability inherent in intimacy.

Fear still pervades the human sexual experience. Its presence is felt in many different forms: shame, guilt, sense of rejection, concern over performance, and doubts about sexual preference. It exists in all of us, for no one escapes his heritage. Sexual fears continue to be a critical part of man's fate because they govern a large segment of his capacity for pleasure.

There are two opposing ways in which we can deal with intense fears. One is through avoidance. In some instances, this is referred to as phobic behavior. The other way is through experiencing and re-experiencing the situation in which the fear occurs, in an effort to convince ourselves it no longer exists. In some cases, this is referred to as counterphobic behavior.

Fear intrudes upon the ability to communicate on any level. Intense fear can make intimate communication impossible. Consequently, for each of us, when the fears that accompany the intimacy inherent in sexual behavior become too great, one cannot effectively participate. One becomes sexually dysfunctional.

The development of technology has made possible the empirical study of the human sexual response, which has given rise to a whole new dimension in medical practice. It is called sex therapy.

Scientific research is now capable of proving to us that about three hundred years ago we were misled by our puritan forefathers. Sex is not an "evil" of the flesh, but an inherent part of human nature. Moreover, sexual behavior cannot simply be explained in terms of lust. It is more complicated than a series of mechanical acts carried out on a bed.

Sex therapists have shown that sexual behavior is essentially a matter of communication. When two people can communicate well together, it usually works. When they can't, it doesn't.

As a result of our better understanding, impotence is no longer viewed medically as a definitive sign of sexual incompetence. Nor is frigidity. Indeed, they can even be signals of a potential for a greater capacity for intimate communication rather than a lesser one. As a matter of fact, the more sensitive a man is, the more vulnerable he is to episodes of impotence. Similarly, the more perceptive and responsive a woman is, the more vulnerable she is to instances of ineffective sexual performance.

Sensitive people are more prone to pick up communicative signals from their partners during the course of lovemaking. These signals are detected whether they were or were not intended to be expressed at that time. Such is the nature of sensitivity. It does not merely serve to pick up the signals we want to receive. It picks up the signals that exist for better or for worse.

For example, the husband who detects hostility in his wife may have difficulty in responding to her with an erection. The hostility may be because of differences in their reactions to a movie or a television show, or a more serious expression of dissension about critical issues in the marriage. Or the hostility may have nothing to do with him at all, but be a residual of other sources of irritation during the course of her day, ranging anywhere from a friend to the grocer. Whatever its cause, hostility clouds the lovemaking atmosphere. It can inhibit a very sensitive man from being able to trust his sexual partner with the vulnerability that he has to expose during lovemaking.

Similarly, a woman may find herself unable to respond to a lover if she detects distraction in him. The distraction may reflect a disinterest in sex at the moment or a preoccupation with a fantasied sexual partner. Her awareness that he is making love to her out of a sense of duty or as a substitute for a more preferred sexual object can make her dysfunctional. Whether she expresses her inability to respond to him by inadequate lubrication or by pain on entry due to contraction of the vaginal muscles or by an inability to achieve orgasm is secondary to her unwillingness to communicate with him intimately.

If the man and woman in these examples did not record the hostility or distraction in their sexual partners, they would not be dysfunctional. Their difficulties came about as a consequence of their sensitivity. Insensitive people are less encumbered. They constitute the sexual athletes in our society. Nothing keeps them from their appointed rounds. They are too insensitive to be sidetracked.

In addition to excessive fear, the egocentricity of narcissistic behavior makes sexual interaction difficult. Narcissistic communication is too one-sided. Moreover, the demands of a narcissist for gratification undermine his willingness to be concerned with the needs of others. In making love, most of his energies are involved with making love to himself. He needs the presence of another's body, but his fantasies during the act of love are generally related to his own.

This is the kind of man who is preoccupied with his own sexual skills and proficiency while making love to someone else. He is busy admiring himself with such thoughts as "I bet she never had anyone who could make love to her this well before" or "I'll get her to have more orgasms in one night than she thought she was capable of." For the narcissist, sexual interaction is always a power struggle from which he must emerge victorious. He must dominate his partner. His pleasure comes more from exclamations of her love for him than it does from any genuine desire to share an intimate experience.

Narcissistic people have difficulty in sustaining relationships. Their attention is always distracted by new fields of conquest. They are always on the make. Their pleasure in sex comes from a constant reaffirmation of their own image. For him, it's a need to be a stud. For her, it's a need to be the best lay in town. Neither is a lover.

Narcissistic lovemaking is becoming increasingly pervasive. Proficiency takes precedence over closeness. Performance takes precedence over intimacy. In the absence of closeness and intimacy, sexual relationships wear thin. Efforts to compensate for growing disinterest encourage experimentation to provide excitement. The use of drugs during the sexual act, extending the relationship to include a third or fourth party, and the use of artificial devices to heighten physical response are all enlisted to maintain interest.

This only contributes to further alienation. Sex is everywhere. Intimacy is harder to find than ever before.

8 /

Masculinity and Femininity:
Social Myths

Sexual roles are more confused today than ever before. The traditional images of masculinity and femininity are under siege.

The female of the species used to be sugar and spice and everything nice. Today she is supposed to be independent, free-thinking, equal to her male peers, and the master of her own fate.

The male of the species used to be rough, tough, and vigorous. Today he is supposed to be sensitive but unthreatened, disciplined but uninhibited, and capable of spontaneous behavior ranging from gentle warmth to impervious commitment to the macho image.

The changing social images for both men and women cause constant conflict. Both groups are polarized by differences in their willingness to accept these changes. There are those who are frightened and cling desperately to the traditional images. There are others who embrace the new sexual models. In both instances, an image rules. What one presents himself or herself as continues to overshadow what one truly is. One and all, we depend on images.

Sexual identity is excessively governed by packaged images. For some, the way to femininity is through the right scent, the right designer clothes, the best coiffure, and being seen in all the "in" places. Others are into the natural look: jeans, T-shirts, no bra, and an occasional live-in boyfriend.

Similarly, masculinity is represented for some by expensive cars, influence in the right places, a wife, kids, and intermittent girlfriends. For others, it is honesty over success, tenderness over strength, and jeans with a collarless shirt rather than the button-down, Ivy League look.

These are extremes of the polarization. Most of us exist—somewhat uncomfortably—in the middle of the spectrum. We commit ourselves to one life style and try to stay abreast of the times by including a little bit from other life styles. For some, however, uncertainty makes it necessary to cover all the bases. Life for them is like having a martini in one hand, a joint in the other, and never being quite sure which is appropriate to the occasion.

No matter what the media may want us to believe, femininity is not acquired through cosmetics, fashion, a provocative figure, a pretty face, bright repartee, or displays of helplessness at the right time. Nor is masculinity to be found at the gym, by paying larger income taxes, or by driving foreign sports cars.

One finds masculinity and femininity only to the extent that he or she can give one's self to another within the structure of a heterosexual relationship. Each of us can give himself, however, only to the extent that he has himself to give.

The more dependent and helpless we feel, the less we are able to share ourselves freely. Our capacity for choosing to be part of a caring relationship is limited by our dependency. Needs born out of feelings of helplessness intrude on our capacities to love.

Choice is the key to finding the highest level of sharing: loving. And independence is the key to the capacity for choice. Only independent people can choose to share their lives. The dependent are forced by their dependency to find someone to lean on.

Among the formidable obstacles that block the way to independence are the sexual roles that were imposed on us as children. In the case of the female of our society, beginning with her childhood, she is traditionally exposed to a program organized around equipping her for her future as a wife and mother. These are the roles held up to her as the avenues that will lead to her identity as a woman. Consequently, she grows up surrounded by dolls with which she is encouraged to play house. Her childhood is designed as a period of rehearsal in play for her future in reality. She is expected to manage her life by making the shift from play to reality. To accomplish this, she is taught that she must attract a man who can provide her with a home and a family.

Beginning with his childhood, the male of our society is also indoctrinated into his future role. In order to assume his posture as the successful breadwinner, he is trained to be aggressive and competitive. For him to achieve that goal, he is encouraged to participate in sports, excel in his studies, and act out certain traditional masculine images, be they superjock or doctor.

These roles were imprinted upon the minds of men and women. They became self-fulfilling prophecies.

The woman comes to believe that it is the duty of the man to provide for her. This, in turn, locks her into a position of dependency on him. She is encouraged to view her personal security as an outgrowth of his protection. Consequently, she learns to live within the framework of a subordinated role. Some women express their dependency submissively by building their lives around their men. Others, equally dependent, rebel and seek to dominate their men as an expression of protest against their assigned female role.

The submissively dependent woman is particularly

attractive to those men who are uncertain and insecure about their own masculinity. For such a man, the dependency of the female gives him a sense of importance and worth. It serves to reduce his doubts about his manliness. Indeed, he relates to her in such a fashion that he constantly reinforces her sense of helplessness. He enjoys the feeling of taking care of her by servicing her helplessness. In such a relationship, if his efforts are passively accepted by the woman, she lives her life in a doll's house in which she assumes the role of the fragile mannequin.

Once she becomes committed to the relationship as the way to guarantee her survival, she is no longer there out of choice. She is bound to the relationship by her well-cultivated helplessness. She lives in the shadow of her man's identity rather than acquiring one of her own, which makes it impossible for her to be free enough to give herself fully to him. Instead, she gives mostly as a means of getting. She learns to please her mate enough to maintain her security. That leaves her with very little in the way of prospects for attaining mature womanhood.

The woman whose dependency is equally real but less apparent seeks a man who needs to lean on her. She looks for someone with a wish to be taken care of. By nurturing him, she is able to dominate him. Then she can mask her own dependency by complaining about the very conditions she has set up. She exploits his vulnerability through a constant barrage of criticism. Her leverage in the relationship is his insecurity. The more uncertain she makes him feel as a man, the greater is his dependency on the relationship. The greater her hold on him, the more she exposes his insecurity. His sense of failure with her forecloses the possibility of leaving to try again with someone else. It is a vicious circle. Her weakness drives her to trade on his weakness. His weakness makes it possible.

Who's Afraid of Virginia Woolf? brilliantly dramatizes the marriage of two people imprisoned by their mutually dependent needs. They constantly assault each other with all forms of verbal and physical abuse; this is accompanied by repeated challenges that the other partner leave the relationship. They accuse each other of being too weak to separate, and each presents himself as the stronger of the two. Both insist that they are staying only because of the extent to which the other one demonstrates his dependence. In reality, both desperately need each other, and their exhibition of abuse is their way of discharging some of their own self-loathing, which stems from their separate feelings of helplessness. In fact, the need of each to use the other as a displaced target for a sense of self-disgust further binds them together. They become dependent on blaming each other for their own personal failures. Unfortunately, *Virginia Woolf* relationships are not restricted to the stage or the screen.

Whether an individual chooses to excessively submit or excessively dominate, he is exercising his dependency. In either instance, he is cheated of the freedom to determine his own fate. His life becomes too connected to the other person.

The women's liberation movement is committed in principle to rectify the stagnant stereotyped roles that have been imposed on women. It is a positive effort to right an ancient wrong. The inalienable right of independence is acknowledged by all. The right of women to pursue their own autonomy is beyond question. The problem lies in paying the price for independence. The Equal Rights Amendment can provide the opportunity, but it cannot guarantee the realization. That is an individual task for men as well as for women.

Like any movement dedicated to change, the women's liberation movement has stirred up a great deal of controversy. Inevitably, it has attracted some women who have exploited the cause as a means of setting up a personal platform. These are the more narcissistic exponents of equal rights who flourish in the bright glow of the media. They constitute a very small number of those who are dedicated to accomplishing progressive change, but their high visibility serves to distort the image of the larger group. These few "showboats" sometimes confuse their personal perspectives with the overall purposes of the movement. They are capable of stirring up so much heat that it masks the light.

The great majority of the women I have encountered who are actively involved in the women's liberation movement are impressive proponents of the opportunity for greater autonomy through self-assertion. They do not discard their female prerogatives by seeking to embrace new sex models or attempt to deny the nature of their biological heritage. They are women, in every sense of the word. They seek not to negate their differences from men, but only the right opportunities equal to those that men enjoy.

To fully realize one's womanliness, one must be willing to forgo nurturing support and be autonomous. To forgo nurturing support, one must be willing to give up the traditional dependent female role in a relationship with a man. This will not be accomplished by demanding women's rights alone. It will be accomplished if women no longer permit themselves to cling to the security of dependent relationships.

I applaud the women's liberation movement, not as a slogan but as a reality. It is crucial to the future of both women and men. It is the means to loving. Loving, in turn, is the way to social survival.

Men have a cross to bear as well. In our society, maleness is expressed much more in terms of an image gained from competing with other men than in behavior that is a direct reflection of relating to women. The tendency is to depict men in such images as the football hero, the all-conquering movie star, the crusading political figure, or the superstud spy of popular literature. The intent is to create an impression of activity and aggression as the male prototype. A more sensitive man often grows up in the face of increasing criticism from male peers who accuse him of being less than a man. He is led to believe that he is manly when he knocks people down and not when he gently helps them up. Warmth, tenderness, and passivity are not part of the macho façade. As a result, young men all too often inhibit their tenderness because of the homosexual anxieties it engenders.

All of us are aware of the type of man with the body beautiful who exudes rippling muscles and embraces a homosexual life, or of the overpowering businessman who dominates the lives of hundreds of employees but is sexually and emotionally impotent with his wife, or of the political leader who exerts great influence in world affairs and cannot assert himself in his marriage.

The measure of a man is not a simple process. It goes far beyond the external trimmings that surround him. It must deal with his ability to sustain an intimate relationship with a woman.

Man's concern about his maleness goes back to the beginnings of recorded history. He has worked so hard to assert his concept of masculinity that one cannot help feeling he does protest too much. Instead of establishing the standards of masculinity in terms of his private behavior in sharing himself with a woman, he demonstrates his maleness by struggling to attain external accomplishments for others to see. He elects to derive his sense of masculinity from without rather than from within.

For the most part, men choose to seek reassurance about their masculinity from other men. So a man takes out as many beautiful women as possible, not just because he is excited by their beauty, but also because it will impress other men. He strives to earn more money than those around him, not merely to enjoy a higher standard of living, but to be able to demonstrate his financial success by driving up to his bigger house, in his more prestigious community, with his more expensive car. He strives to master athletic skills, not only because he enjoys playing the games, but because he can then be seen competitively defeating other men.

It is interesting to note that the very qualities men use to establish manliness appear to be more homosexual than heterosexual. They involve winning recognition from other men by surpassing them, rather than by succeeding at sustaining a communicative relationship with a woman. The fact is that all men maintain relationships with other men. They provide the opportunity for self-expression, a part of which is obtained from friendly competition. This does not brand men as being homosexuals. Ultimately, the measure of maleness will come only from the extent to which men are able to sustain a communicative relationship with a woman.

Homosexuality has received a great deal of attention lately. There has been a visible increase in its number. Some people feel that this is a result of the greater acceptance of homosexuality in our society, which has encouraged more homosexuals to come out into the open. The shift in our social attitudes is reflected by the official change in the position of the American Psychiatric Association, which no longer designates homosexuality as a mental illness.

The nature of mental illness would have to lend itself to a more precise definition in order to warrant the inclusion of homosexuality. But there is no issue relative to regarding homosexuality as a social dysfunction insofar as it undermines the potential for the survival of the species. In terms of individual dysfunction, however, it would have to be evaluated with

regard to the extent to which it represents a pathologi-
cal avoidance of women.

I believe that there is an increase in the number of
homosexuals in our society and that this increase reflects the increase in narcissism. Narcissists are more
prone to love others like themselves.

The level of narcissism in homosexuals is generally
high. They tend to be the more stylish and image-
oriented within any social group. They dominate the
image-making industries: design, fashion, and the arts.

For some, the homosexual preference is determined
genetically. They are born with ambiguous biological
identities. Their biochemical makeup does not support
their external genitalia. From early childhood on, these
individuals manifest behavior that is different from that
of other children of the same sex. They may move
differently, posture themselves differently, talk differently, pursue different interests, or simply stand away
from the rest of the group. Through chemical assays
of the androgen-estrogen balance in their body, the
nature of their differences can sometimes be explained.

For most homosexuals, however, theirs is a choice
born of fear. They withdraw from the frightening demands of a relationship with someone of the opposite
sex and move into relationships with others who mirror
themselves. The very act of choosing another who
physically duplicates one's self increases the narcissistic
quality of the relationship.

All of us have doubts about our sexuality. They are
often expressed as homosexual anxieties. The existence
of fears about one's sexual identity does not make one
a homosexual. Homosexuality involves a choice characterized by preference for someone of the same sex.
It is not enough to fear that no one of the opposite
sex will be willing to have you. Whether the opposite
sex wants you or not, it must be clearly established that
you don't want them as sexual partners.

Man has found it necessary to distort the capability of women. He invented the myth that women constituted the "weaker sex," which allowed him to identify himself as the "stronger sex."

In fact, the data of human experience does not substantiate that women are weaker in any regard except possibly muscle mass. They are as bright or brighter, tend to live longer than men, and have demonstrated the ability to master the skills and vocational endeavors traditionally considered the exclusive domains of men. In terms of sexual capacity and potential, they are superior to men.

Man must have always understood and feared that greater sexual capacity of women, else why his need to create an elaborate myth designed to disinterest them in their sexual potential? This was apparently his way of protecting himself from anticipated sexual demands that he felt he could not fulfill.

Throughout history women have been led to believe that sex was a male prerogative. Men trained them to reject and deny their own sexual impulses. Women learned to inhibit even their awareness of sexual feelings. Consequently, they educated themselves not to look for much pleasure in this critical area of human experience. The feminine role was structured so that a woman gave herself sexually to a man in exchange for the security provided through marriage. She was discouraged from making sexual demands of a man and was taught to respond passively to his demands. Sex was his prerogative, not hers.

With the advent of modern psychology, women were educated to understand their potential capacity for pleasure through sexual expression. They were encouraged to be more expressive about their sexual interests. They were made aware that it was all right to make demands on men for sexual gratification. They learned that it was permissible to initiate sexual activity to pursue their own particular preferences in lovemaking. They were advised to give up their passive inhibitions and seek sexual fulfillment.

To some extent, this has come as a jolt to men. As women have become freer, men have become less able to function with them. This is particularly true with the young. The heightened receptivity and sexual interest of young women has brought an increase in transient episodes of impotence among young men. Young women report that it is not at all uncommon for their men to have premature ejaculations or experience instances of an inability to have or sustain an erection.

Interestingly enough, young women do not view impotence with the same degree of alarm as their parents did. They do not regard it as a signal of serious masculine dysfunction, but as a temporary reaction to a new lovemaking situation. The women report that they deal with it by being gentle, comforting, and reassuring. They find that as the man gets over his performance anxieties, the problem usually disappears.

Impotence is now endemic among the young. It appears to be a common reaction to the relatively new demands placed on men by women. It was one thing for a young man in the 1940s to get a woman to submit to him because of his imagined prowess. It is quite another thing to be confronted with a woman who initiates sexual intimacy with the implicit demand that he give her satisfaction and pleasure. Such candor on the part of women leaves little room for illusions of masculinity derived from the old images. Men must instead come to terms with their heightened vulnerability relative to the superior capacity of women.

Indeed, recent empirical studies of orgasmic capacity clearly establish the greater potential of women over men. During lovemaking, women can have multiple orgasms within the same time that men have a single ejaculation. Moreover, they can have sexual intercourse more frequently than men within a given period of time. This is a biological reality; no man can totally match the sexual potential of a woman.

The point here is not to establish that women are superior to men, but rather to expose the myths about their weakness. They are neither weaker nor stronger. They are different.

All too frequently, sexual behavior becomes a power struggle. Who is in charge becomes more important than intimate communication. Only by each individual's accepting his own sexual role can the competitive struggle be avoided. The acceptance of one's sexual role is an inherent part of establishing an independent sense of self. This is equally true for men and for women. If either partner seeks to be superior to the other, both will lose.

Life is crowded by conflict. We live in a gray world most of the time, where pleasure is restricted by the need for social compromise. Pleasure is what makes the price worth paying.

Sex is paramount in our pursuit of pleasure. Not sex as a mechanistic, narcissistic performance in order to establish a sense of mastery over the sexual act, but sex as an intimate, sharing experience that exposes our vulnerabilities. It enables us to convert these vulnerabilities from a source of fear to a source of joy. It defeats loneliness by permitting fuller communication.

A woman once told me that she discovered her femininity by understanding her man's vulnerabilities and no longer having the need to take advantage of them. Her man might well say that with her help, he discovered his masculinity by accepting his vulnerabilities.

9 /

The Failure of Marriage

We should marry only as a commitment to loving. Marital love is the prototype for all other forms of loving in the society. Consequently, there is no behavioral pattern more critical to man's survival.

Most married people love each other. The problem —and it is a tragic one—is that very few are still in love with each other. The relationship usually loses the quality of romance.

In marriage, romance becomes obsolete as responsibilities for children and the home intrude upon what was once an idyllic relationship. It is a difficult loss for the marital partners to face, so they deal with it by denial and by focusing instead on the self-sacrificing role of parenthood.

Children are an extension of parental love but must always be subordinated to it. In a healthy family structure, the child should recognize that his parents' loyalty and affection for each other take precedence over their feelings for him. He will accept his "second best" status, however, only after he experiences consistent failure in his efforts to intrude upon the parental relationship.

The child grows to admire, take pride in, and envy

his parents' love for each other. But his "second best" status also serves as a source of displeasure to him, and it will ultimately motivate him to search outside the home for a relationship like the one his parents enjoy. Then, like his parents before him, he can come first in a loving marital relationship of his own. He, too, will defend his marriage from intrusions that would dilute the love between him and his wife, no less effectively than his parents protected theirs from him.

When the committed loving relationship between parents can be sustained, it serves as the ideal for which the child strives as an adult. On the other hand, if he succeeds in coming between his parents and they subordinate their feelings for each other to their feeling for him, his image of marriage becomes far less than an ideal worth pursuing during adulthood. In either instance, what the child learns about the nature of love in his own household, he will carry with him for the rest of his life.

As adolescents, we are encouraged to pursue more intimate relationships. Since adolescence is regarded as a period of apprenticeship in our society, the teenager is given the luxury of forming such relationships without paying the price inherent in caring for another. He is permitted free and relatively uninhibited range to experience the joy and intensity of his first romantic involvement. He is offered a way of rehearsing for adulthood by passing through a transitional period of life when he is able to feel love for another without having to deal with the demands of commitment. He is still permitted to live with his parents and be dependent on them to provide him with most necessities.

In entering a loving relationship, adolescents are not burdened with the need to assume the responsibility for each other's daily needs. They are able to dedicate themselves totally to romance as an end in itself. They can enjoy the illusion of living for each other by virtue of being relieved of any of the harsh realities of having to provide for their mate.

This is not meant as an indictment of adolescent romance. It is simply a realistic description of the state of affairs during that period of life. One of the great privileges of adolescence is the right to experience highly charged and emotionally consuming romances. There is an aesthetic quality to such love that most adults, unfortunately, lose and never recapture.

For those adolescents who pass through their teenage years without experiencing this heightened sense of living, one can only feel a deep sense of regret. Once the impact of competitive adult realities takes over, it doesn't come easily again.

The adolescent is free to experience intense episodes of narcissistic love. His relationships are unencumbered and untested by the impact of time and reality. He can indulge himself in repeated encounters by having illusions of idyllic mating, the perfect match between totally compatible lovers. He can soar when his romances are in full bloom, and loudly bemoan his fate when he crashes each time the bubble bursts.

No time of life is so persistently volatile as adolescence. The volatility reflects the narcissism. Life for the young is a roller coaster, alternating between incredible highs and devastating lows. The intensity of their reactions reflects their self-centeredness; almost everything that goes on in their lives takes on life-or-death meaning. Their heightened narcissism, by definition, makes anything that is related to them a matter of importance.

Anyone who has ever lived in the same household with adolescents knows the extent to which their presence dominates it. Their preoccupation with themselves becomes exasperating to other members of the family. They monopolize the telephone. They linger repeatedly and endlessly in front of the bathroom mirror. Their interests overwhelm anyone else's: their music blares; their posters, school banners, and pinups decorate the walls; their sports equipment clutters the closets, and their favorite health foods crowd the pantry. When they are around, everybody knows it. Their narcissism rules the roost, as they utilize this time of their lives to make the important decisions that will shape their futures. As far as they are concerned, the others who live at home will just have to grin and bear it.

Love always begins as an illusion. By falling in love with the image of a person before we can know his true substance, we assign him qualities we want to believe he has. In that way we can think of the person in terms that enhance our own lives. And so it should be.

Our sexual relationships start with a mutual attraction. They begin because we like what we see. We are attracted by an image we are exposed to. The image is more than someone's physical appearance; it includes the style and manner with which he displays himself. After the initial attraction, we set out on a campaign to win his interest and affection. To accomplish this, we present ourselves as the kind of person we believe the other wants—we tell stories we think he wants to hear, profess interest in the things he says he likes, dress to please him, and defer to him. We do everything to ingratiate ourselves:

"Where do you want to go?"

"Anywhere you'd like to take me."

"I'll take you any place you'd like to go."

"I'll go anywhere as long as you take me."

And on and on. Ideally, with time, we become more honest with each other. Each is better able to offer the other the opportunity to know him as he truly is. This situation always contains a double-edged sword. On the one hand, it enables us to relax in the relationship and be ourselves. On the other hand, we run the risk of tarnishing the shining image we have worked so hard to create.

All of us live with some doubts about our lovability. To some extent, we are afraid of revealing our more narcissistic inner faces, fearing that it will make us unlovable. Feelings of unlovability drive us to retain our superficial poses, and limit the degree to which we will permit ourselves to be loved for ourselves. As a result, a certain amount of deception exists in every relationship. The more secure the partners, the greater their capacity to share themselves in open and honest terms. Their openness is measured by their ability to communicate through feelings as well as thoughts. Each new exposure that is accepted by a lover makes possible more exposures. In time, we become free to reveal our liabilities as well as our assets.

Marriage should combine the exquisite excitement of adolescent narcissistic romance with the ability to assume the responsibility involved in caring for each other. It is a fusion of illusion and reality, an intermingling of narcissistic love and a more sharing love for another human being. The absence of either of these qualities makes the relationship incomplete. These loving qualities supplement each other. Together, they sharpen the sense of fulfillment loving gives us. Narcissistic love is the spice of loving; a more sharing love is its substance.

Tracing the natural history of a marriage is the best means of clarifying these two forms of love. To a significant degree, each of us begins by marrying an illusion. We enter into a life that promises to provide a highly exciting and strongly desired relationship with another human being who represents, in part at least, the fulfillment of some longed-for fantasy. Initially, the illusory quality dominates the character of the relationship regardless of the amount of time that was devoted to getting to know each other during the courtship.

This is a time of wistful daydreaming about children

not yet born and houses not yet constructed. It is a hand-holding time when we enjoy many beautiful moments furnishing our castles in the air. It is a time when our hopes are boundless, and we live with the conviction that, without doubt, no one has ever loved quite as we do.

All too soon relationships begin to feel the impact of intrusive responsibilities. The husband becomes preoccupied with his need to make enough money to build his castle in the air. The demands of his professional and business activities consume his time and energy. He indulges less in the pleasures of romance. Similarly, his wife becomes interested in establishing the kind of home that expresses her identity. She works to provide her conception of a more desirable climate to support the marital relationship and to deal with the requirements of raising children.

Both lose a little of their perspective as they become more and more involved with things rather than with each other. The dimensions of security come to take on greater meaning than before. As the partners accumulate more, there is more to protect. There is concern about the risk of loss, which is no longer confined to each other.

They begin to expand the space they require in order to live together. From the intimacy of a studio apartment to the spaciousness of a one-bedroom apartment. Then two. Then three. Then a den, wood-burning fireplaces, a separate dining room. . . .

Finally, the most significant intrusion of all arrives— the birth of their child. Children are fulfilling dimensions in life, but they also exact a great price. They intrude irrevocably upon the romantic dimensions of a marriage. No more casual lovemaking. No freedom to come and go as we please. Home-cooked gourmet meals may give way to TV dinners because of the fatigue of child rearing, and conversation becomes self-conscious because another person is present. The impact of the added responsibility is felt in both the bedroom and the bankbook. The lovers have become parents.

In any marriage, as the commitment to children increases and the romance diminishes, the vicious cycle begins. The more the presence of the child intrudes, the greater the shift of emphasis. The heightened burden of responsibility suffocates the idyllic quality of love. The loss of this narcissistic excitement increases the commitment to real and imagined duty. And accompanying this is a loss of pleasure.

It is important to deal honestly with the realities imposed on a marriage by the decision to have a child. Especially since all too often the choice whether or not to have a child is an abortive one. In too many cases, parents are responding to pressures exerted by forces outside the marriage that lead them to feel they are expected to have children, rather than carefully examining the unique position that a child would assume in their own marriage. One should not have a child merely to fit into the conventional frame of reference.

In my introduction to this book, I indicated that living was easier when one's goals dealt primarily with the issue of survival. When our survival is relatively secure, however, life gets far more complicated as the luxury of security allows us to reach out for pleasure. The more pleasure we pursue, the more complex our lives will be. Moreover, if the pursuit of pleasure is not buffered by the requirements of social restraint, we jeopardize the very security that enabled us to seek more pleasure in the first place. As we return to gratifying more of our natural narcissistic wants, we compromise the viability of our society, the same society that underwrote our security by protecting us from a life where only the fittest would survive.

This dynamic also holds true in marriage. Seeking a relationship primarily for purposes of security makes for a less complicated life. The marriage has a better chance to survive because the marital partners are not demanding the highest possible levels of pleasure from the relationship. They seek a stable commitment to a caring friendship rather than the broad fulfillment of personal fantasies. They do not bring much narcissistic love to their relationship to begin with. Consequently, there is no serious risk to the marriage from the loss of romance; it didn't significantly exist in the first place. In such a marriage, the birth of a child is far less intrusive.

The risk is greatest for those who seek the highest ideal—total fulfillment through love. As in any other situation, the greater the return, the greater the risk. All of us must decide the way we want to conduct our lives. If we want to play it safe, we opt for the more conservative marriage anchored in security. Life may be duller, but it is easier. If we want to go for broke, we have to take our chances. There will be more uncertainty about obtaining our goal. Our life may be fuller, but it is harder. The excitement and fulfillment of a life that is organized around an optimal blending of narcissistic love and a more sharing love cannot provide the safety and serenity found in a life that is anchored around the security of a more sharing love relatively devoid of the narcissistic quality of romance.

That is why living was "easier in the old days." There was more insecurity about survival, so more people opted for the kind of life that offered less. Marriages were frequently matches negotiated exclusively in terms of practical realities; there was little room for illusion and fantasy. Marriages negotiated by matchmakers had a higher survival rate than marriages consummated on the wings of romance. The matchmaker's marital partners more readily found what they bargained for—security.

So the decision about children must reflect the couple's broader goals in life. Children are always intrusive, but much more so with regard to the narcissistic component of a loving relationship. They are a risk to marital partners primarily to the extent that the partners are unwilling to give up the romance in their lives. It is not a case of one life style being right and the other being wrong. Each of us has the right to shape his own life. What we must determine is what we feel is right for us, knowing in advance that there is no way for us to have it all.

All of us crave some narcissistic fulfillment. As a secondary component of human experience, it provides the opportunity to enjoy some of our childhood residuals during the course of an effective adult life. There is a boy in every man, a girl in every woman, and it is not the purpose of maturity to destroy this charming quality. Indeed, the child who resides within us adds color and dimension to our adult lives. It is a problem only when the childish part of our adult makeup persists as the dominant force in our behavior.

Narcissistic love reflects our childish wish to be special. It deals with the desire to "be the best" by extending this longing into the marriage through the fantasy that "our love is greater than any other." It permits marital partners to think of each other as the most caring, the most considerate, the most sensitive, the best lover, the best dancer. It makes it possible to think of a beautiful lovemaking experience not only as an extremely compatible episode of shared communicative intimacy, but also as a complete fusion of two bodies into one. It converts the sensuality of sharing a fine bottle of wine or a good meal into a love ritual designed to phase out the rest of the world as the lovers prepare to devour each other. It converts a walk into a promenade, and jogging before breakfast into an exhilarating exploration of the morning air. It makes the totality of living a part of the foreplay between lovers.

As a secondary component of marriage, narcissistic

love clearly breeds romance. It adds some fantasy to living, which helps to buffer the demanding realities of life. But there is a difference between living in reality while supplementing it with fantasy and living in fantasy while supplementing it with reality.

It is not by chance that I referred to narcissistic love as the spice of life. Spice is only a seasoning added to a much larger mass of food for flavor; too much ruins the taste of the food that it was intended to improve.

Such is the nature of narcissistic love. Small amounts enhance the quality of loving within a marriage. Too much will destroy the marriage itself.

Too few of us reach the highest levels of loving. Too few of us reach the level of autonomy necessary to be able to love fully. Too few of us can supplement the narcissistic quality of romance in a relationship with intimate trust born of shared vulnerability.

Those few who do attain the quality of loving that reflects full and compatible communication share a demanding responsibility—protection of the precious level of human experience that they have achieved. In this regard, the intrusion of a child is a serious danger for them.

This is not intended as an argument against having children. It is meant to suggest that those few who reach the level of independence and emotional maturity at which they are able to share themselves almost totally with another human being should carefully weigh the decision to have children. If living is about loving, it makes no sense to forfeit the goal once it is attained.

It is ironic that those who love best—and would therefore make the best parents—have the most to lose from the presence of children in their lives. Fortunately, however, in terms of the fate of mankind, only a limited few realize the level of loving that makes a child a liability to the marital relationship. For most of us, children contribute more to our lives than they take away. The only time a child takes more than he brings is when the parents have so much between them that their relationship will not be enhanced by his presence.

Even when adults have succeeded in loving each other at the highest levels, they may knowingly choose to have a child. Such a choice would reflect their willingness to forgo some of the qualities in their relationship in favor of parenthood. This is particularly relevant to the desire of some women to fulfill themselves by bearing a child. It is part of the innate biology of women that makes them different from men. A loving husband may want to provide his wife with such self-fulfillment out of the very feelings of love that he recognizes will be compromised by her bearing a child. But the incredible creative force that the capacity to bear a child represents cannot be underestimated. It is a unique potential that is difficult for a woman to deny totally. Indeed, some argue that the fact that most creative art forms have been dominated by men throughout history reflects man's need to compensate for his inability to give birth to a child.

The realistic demands of contained closeness as a result of sharing the same living space also put pressure on marriages, even when they are extensions of the most ideal forms of loving relationships. It takes constant effort to sustain the high level of the loving commitment between marital partners. The necessary balance between the romantic narcissistic component and the dominant component of more shared love in their relationship is a very sensitive one; it requires constant monitoring to preserve. External forces are always threatening to throw the communicative interaction out of balance. The need for vigilance is endless. Good things just don't come easily.

The key to maintaining the quality of a loving relationship lies in policing the narcissistic component, for it is the more unstable one. It is constantly threatening to erupt and challenge the more shared loving aspect of a relationship for dominance. Fortunes of fate, such as a sudden, unexpected rush of success or a crippling accident, can increase the narcissism of one of the partners to the point where he is no longer predominately being a more sharing lover.

I know of the case of a young English teacher who enjoyed a marvelous loving relationship with his wife. She was an independent young woman who pursued her own interests and her own career in the course of sharing herself fully with her husband. Her love for him enabled him to be more assertive in expressing himself creatively. He undertook the writing of a novel, armed with her encouragement.

In its initial form, the book was rejected by several publishers. He was greatly disappointed, but, buffered by her love, he rewrote the manuscript. It was then accepted for publication contingent on his willingness to tour the country for six weeks in order to help sell the book. His wife's independent work responsibilities made it impossible for her to join him. It was their first period of sustained separation.

Deprived of the opportunity for communication that her physical presence provided, he compensated by investing all his energies in the tour. This contributed to help make the book a huge success.

His life changed. The successful first book brought lucrative offers to write more books. He was courted by agents and lawyers. He gave up teaching and devoted most of his time to writing. His success grew; he became a man of means with power and a public identity.

His relationship with his wife faltered, however. He continued to love her, but not in the same way. His successful career dominated their lives, as did his narcissism that followed in its wake. After not too long a time, his wife decided that she was unwilling to settle for less than she had had, and she left the relationship.

It is of no consequence to try to fix blame in this example. The point is that a uniquely rich and fulfilling loving relationship was lost by two people, neither of whom had ever intended to compromise it. The destruction of the marriage was not premeditated. In many ways, it was an accident of fate. Nevertheless, both partners ended up as losers. They had reached a special place in life but could not hold on to it.

The writer subsequently felt that he had lost more than he had gained. He has never been able to replace the relationship that he once enjoyed with his wife. According to him, the reason is because he had changed. He was unable to control the growth of his narcissism in the wake of his success. It made loving as he had experienced it before impossible for him. He feels that if he had it to do over again, he would gladly forgo his success as a writer if he could relive the love he had known.

The story is a humbling one. It dramatizes the difficulty in keeping our narcissistic balance in the face of events that continually invite the expression of narcissism. None of us is immune; none of us can qualify to cast the first stone at our fellow man who has lost his way. Such arrogance would betray the fact that we had already lost control of our own narcissism.

In light of the precarious nature of sustaining love on its highest levels, some parents elect to pursue a less risky life style. They do this totally aware that they are giving up some of the fullness that exists in their relationship. They can decide to have a child as a means of assisting them to control the narcissism in each other. That is one of the ways in which a child contributes to a household. The reality of his presence and the demands he imposes by virtue of his needs to be taken care of serve to limit the prospects for excessive flights into narcissistic fancy on the part of his parents.

We will always strive to express our narcissism on some level. When it can no longer be discharged within the romantic dimensions of the husband-wife relationship owing to the presence of a child, we will seek it elsewhere, most commonly in the very objects that took it from us in the first place: our children. We can live vicariously through their accomplishments and bask in the glory of their successes. We can utilize them as extensions of the unfulfilled parts of ourselves. Obviously, this is not in our best interest; nor is it in theirs.

As another alternative, we might turn our attention to the accumulation of power. Power is gained through building an empire of personal prestige, wealth, or political influence. But power further corrupts our capacity to care and drives us more deeply into an uncaring way of life. It pushes us into a primarily narcissistic life style. It stimulates much more narcissism than that which serves to spice the life of the more loving person; it creates a pervasive narcissistic force that is destructive to loving itself.

We must resolve the dilemma for ourselves. Do we have children or do we not? Children take away the narcissistic pleasure of romance. But in forcing us to take on responsibility, they also protect us from being overwhelmed by our narcissism. Without children, the more narcissistic can lose their way, drifting into excessive self-gratification. On the other hand, if one is committed to the highest level of loving, there is little room for a child.

Within the context of social living there is no substitute for love. The further man is driven from a loving posture, the more destructive he is to himself and others. He invariably increases his narcissistic orientation and becomes less and less able to share, at a time when sharing is more critical than ever to mankind's survival.

Marriage is the most effective social structure in which love can be experienced. It is toward this end that it must be maintained. When it is corrupted by an insatiable hunger for security and power, the meaning of the relationship is destroyed not only for the marriage partners but also for the children. The marital interaction is the model on which each child molds his own capacity to love.

All too often marriage is viewed as a bond that has to survive for the sake of survival itself. This is defended by the rationalization that by maintaining constancy in the family structure, the children are better served. This has not proved to be the case. Marriages kept together solely for the sake of children function to distort the child's conception of himself and of life in general. Marriage, like any other social institution, should survive only as long as it enhances the partners' self-realization. When it is no longer an avenue for loving, its existence as an end in itself cannot be defended.

In the musical *Fiddler on the Roof*, there is a moment when the beleaguered and burdened husband turns to his wife and asks, "Do you love me?" Her response is that she cannot understand why he questions whether she loves him, since for twenty years she has done his laundry, washed his floors, and tended his children. But this does not adequately define marital love. It does signify that by virtue of the duties that have been shared together, and through the trust and friendship that have grown out of common effort, the partners feel love for each other. It does not, however, show in any significant way that they are or ever were romantically in love with each other; or that they ever were capable of sharing a more independent loving relationship.

There is no substitute for independently loving and being in love with another human being. When you possess it in a marriage, you should not let anything intrude to undermine the integrity of such caring. Its existence is vital in order to preserve the ideal of self-fulfillment within the social framework of the human condition.

10 /

Power: The Alternative Life Style

Power always corrupts. Power is an interest in exercising control over others. It seeks to manipulate the response of others by directing them toward an action desired by the person in power. It is diametrically opposed to free choice. It deals with sharing only to the extent that the sharing does not dilute the primary purpose for which power is accumulated: the control of others.

Narcissism breeds power, and power breeds narcissism. Each exists because of the other, and both serve to make each other grow.

Power is the avenue through which the narcissist's demands for pleasurable self-fulfillment can be imposed on others. It ensures the fulfillment of his dependent wishes and enables him to barter favor in exchange for nurturing and gratification.

But uneasy lies the head that wears the crown; the king of the hill is always fair game. His power is always in jeopardy. The more he wields it to enhance his life, the more vulnerable he is to being unable to survive without it.

Power is elusive; it is impossible to possess absolutely. It can be retained only for fleeting moments. It is always on the verge of vanishing. Consequently the pursuit of power is relentless because it is constantly fueled by the fear that it will disappear and bring the inevitable fall. The higher one gets, the greater the anticipation of the fall.

Those without power seek it in the hope that it will provide the security they lack. They conceive of power as a finite thing that is controllable, but power is uncontrollable. It is a parasitic monster that feeds on itself. The problem is that its dimensions are infinite; there always seems to be another level to attain. The quest to reach a plateau where there is no one to answer to is an endless one; there is always someone to answer to.

The more power one has, the greater the need to hold on to it—and the greater the fear of losing it. More and more energy must be invested to ensure one's self against falling from the grace of power. There are potential successors everywhere. One must guard in all directions at all times. The concerns of self-protection are all-consuming. Everyone is a possible conspirator; no one is above suspicion. This state leaves little room for friendships and family. Most important of all, there can be no real commitment to a loving relationship.

What, then, makes power so attractive to so many? Why are so many human moths consumed by its flames? Why so many attempts to reach a point from which there is obviously no return? The extent to which each of us seeks power is a measure of one's narcissism. Because narcissism is a universal force, each of us pursues power to some degree.

Loving is diametrically opposed to power. It intrudes upon narcissism by rendering us vulnerable to those we love. It exposes us to the endless barrage of the needs—both expressed and unexpressed—of someone other than ourselves. Loving forces us to subvert some of our own demands for gratification to the requirements of another. There is no way a loving partner can reign supreme. He is always subject to the scrutiny of the communicative demands inherent in a loving relationship.

By definition, loving and power are incompatible. The energies consumed by one are invariably diverted from the other. More love, less power; more power, less love.

This is a reality few of us are willing to face, preferring to live with the illusion that we can have the best of both worlds. Nevertheless, at some time in our lives we must inevitably face the same kind of choices as *The Man in the Gray Flannel Suit,* a loving marital partner who began to accumulate power. At first he ignored the complaints of his wife as he responded to the narcissistic excitement of his success. His rationalization was that everything he was doing was done only in order to provide greater material security for his family. The increasing demands of his success, however, ultimately brought him to the moment of truth. He was forced to face the reality that less and less time and energy were available for loving. He had to choose between the narcissistic gratifications afforded by the power he was gaining in his career and the pleasures of a sharing love with his wife. He had more strength than most of us. He chose loving.

Narcissism is an addictive force. In fact, all forms of addiction are expressions of narcissism. Whether it be heroin or chocolate candy, it is the narcissistic pleasure that we become addicted to. The "drug" an addict chooses is only the means to the end. The end is relief from the pain of the constant stream of deprivation that accompanies reality in favor of the narcissistic gratifications gained through self-indulgence. All addictions are narcissistic disorders and all addicts are narcissists.

Like any other form of narcissistic behavior, power is addictive. We acquire the habit over a long period of time by permitting ourselves to succumb to steadily increased dosages. We graduate from the part-time secretary loaned from the typing pool to a full-time secretary of our own. Then on to the executive bathroom and the carpeted office floors, from the back of the plane to the first-class cabin, from the bus to the taxi to the limousine. Pretty soon it's the only way to go. It's more than a kick; it becomes a way of life. We're hooked.

Once we are addicted, cure is improbable. As with any form of addiction, the successful cure rate is very low. Periods of remission are possible, but the craving persists.

Executive suites are the nemesis of loving partners. They are filled with senior executives who are assigned to act as the "pushers" to make "junkies" out of the junior executives. Once addicted, the junior executives, in turn, become the pushers who addict others.

The corporation has many drugs that it can hook you with. First and foremost is money. Next comes prestige through position. Then there is a long succession of what the corporate world calls perks; these include everything from the best table in a popular restaurant to tickets, to the hottest show in town, a special parking place, or even sex on the expense account. They all act as booster doses to keep the habit growing.

It is never painless to give up any form of narcissistic pleasure, and the pursuit of power is no exception to the rule. But it can be done as long as we have not yet allowed ourselves to become addicted. There is always a period during which the choice to recommit ourselves to a life of more shared loving remains viable. There comes a critical point, however, where choice is no longer possible. Whether or not we'll recognize that point in time depends on how long we go on kidding ourselves into believing that we can enjoy the best of both worlds—hold on to our loving relationships while increasing our base of power. Some of us wait too long before we allow ourselves to recognize the extent to which we have withdrawn personal energies from our loved ones to ourselves, as we shift our priorities from the loving relationship to our career.

The use of the executive suite is but one illustration of power. It can be more subtly accumulated. There are other ways to manipulate and control people. Lawyers, doctors, teachers, clergymen, journalists, and politicians exert great influence over others. Indeed, these professions may not be as high-paying as careers in the business world, but they are attractive to many because they provide greater opportunity for narcissistic rewards—in terms of social prestige and in manipulative influence upon people.

The ability to go from rags to riches is part of the American Dream. The opportunity to move up the social scale is a quality of our society in which we take pride. It is a unique strength in our national way of life. But it also creates a great deal of individual turbulence. On the positive side, the high degree of upward mobility, where anyone can be President, is a tribute to our free society. On the negative side, the very fact that it is possible for everyone to become a millionaire increases his narcissistic vulnerability. It requires that each of us has the strength to make choices about options that other societies do not offer. There are more narcissistic alternatives available that have to be dealt with.

Success is glorified in our society. Consequently, the successful are often exalted as ideals. The reality is that our powerful celebrities usually live far less than ideal lives. Their stature creates a constant struggle to maintain a realistic sense of identity.

The most severe form of identity loss occurs to the person who lives out the Horatio Alger story in his own life. By advancing far beyond his origins, he becomes extremely vulnerable to "boot-strap" disease—having "pulled himself up by his boot straps" to a station in life that is far beyond the position he started from, he lives with the fear that he will lose it all and be forced back to the point from which his climb originally began. If the distance that he has come is far enough, he views the fall back as an endless descent. It is as if the rug he is standing on will be pulled out from under him and he will be left with nothing.

In our success-oriented culture, winning, rather than sharing, is the name of the game. Success is so all-encompassing that we live with a phobic avoidance of failure. We pursue only those activities in which we can assure ourselves of a successful outcome.

In such a life, the meaning of pleasure becomes distorted. The fear of failure is so great, we live almost constantly with a form of anxiety that can be relieved only by some type of successful accomplishment. The anxiety about failure is so persistent in our lives that when it is not present, we regard our state as pleasurable. In this manner, pleasure becomes distorted to mean the absence of pain. But pleasure is not merely the absence of the negative; it is a positive state in its own right, occurring when we are able to express our inner needs through socially acceptable behavior.

It is unfortunate that we have such a great fear of failure, because it is success that is far more dangerous to the human condition. Failure bruises and smarts, but success can devastate. Failure attacks our self-esteem and can cause depression. Success excites narcissism and creates such emotional highs that communication becomes impossible. Psychiatrically it is far easier to treat the bruises and depression of failure than the narcissistic inflation of success.

The narcissistic child is addicted very early to successful performance. He learns not to permit himself to respond spontaneously to stimulation. He disciplines himself to react only to those things that promise success. He selectively develops those skills that protect him from failure. He prefers activities that he can master through practice. Personal feelings cannot be readily controlled or practiced, so close relationships are avoided because they stir up feelings. This makes for a loveless life, and he compensates by seeking power.

It would be ludicrous to indict all success. We all pursue it to some extent. It can enrich our lives and contribute to our sense of worth. The issue is how much of it works best for each of us. Too little may not be enough to give us the self-esteem necessary to expose ourselves to the vulnerability of caring; too much may ferment narcissism to the extent that caring becomes impossible.

How can we determine the amount of success that we can tolerate? When is it too much? What are the warning signs?

The measurement always deals with the balance between narcissism and loving. If a given success increases our ability to love, it is certainly not too much. However, if it increases our self-centeredness and reduces our desire to care, it is too much. Each of us must take measure of himself, daily, venture by venture, thought by thought. It is sad to witness the erosion of a loving human being by success. The insidious nature by which it overtakes the capacity to care is astonishing. It intrudes in small ways at first, takes its toll slowly, and, if unchecked, takes over completely.

With success come the rewards. Slowly at first, but they grow, and soon the neighbors begin to take notice. You can get a table at the better restaurants. People defer to you and seek your counsel. The prestige and possessions of your wife and children increase. So does your sense of self. Finally, you begin to think of yourself as special. From there on, it's downhill all the way.

If the narcissistic expansion is great enough, you no longer merely talk; you drop pearls of wisdom. You no longer have time for small pleasures; you're too busy moving mountains. Casual dinner invitations from friends must be responded to selectively—who else is on the guest list? You no longer rap easily with your kids; you offer sermons from the mount of fatherhood instead. Admission to previously inaccessible places is now possible; you have connections and influence. You have moved from the humility born out of caring and loving into the self-inflated regions of arrogance and grandiosity.

I recall the effects of success on the owner of a moderately sized family business whose company was bought by a large conglomerate. As one of the conditions of the sale, he was required to take a management position in the broadly diversified parent corporation. This made it necessary for him to travel regularly throughout the world to attend corporate meetings.

Previously, he had been a family man who lived modestly. He had inherited the traditions of a disciplined and frugal New England life style from his father. He was raised to regard extravagance as foolishness and self-praise as weakness.

His new role as an executive of a powerful international organization changed all that. Instead of flying coach as he always had in the past, he was now provided with first-class travel accommodations. Limousines replaced taxis, hotel suites replaced single rooms. At first the changes were a novelty, but they soon became part of his way of life. He began to require such luxuries on his personal trips as well; he was not able to confine the superfluous trappings of his success to his business world.

He spent more and more time away from his family, at first under protest, but soon by choice. Finally, during a business meeting abroad, he casually admired an extraordinarily beautiful woman in a restaurant and was later surprised to find her waiting for him at his hotel. She had been bought and paid for by his associate. The incident marked the transformation of the New England country gentleman to the swinging conglomerate officer.

It was only a matter of time before there was no turning back. He lost the conservative identity that had been cultivated by his family for generations and became an expansive, self-indulgent imitation of an uninhibited playboy. The transition, however, was only an applied veneer to his traditional core, which had been too well ingrained to be changed easily.

I met him after he had become an alcoholic. He was drinking excessively because he couldn't find his way back to himself. He had been using alcohol in his unsuccessful attempts to dull the depression caused by his loss of identity.

All of us have moments when we do not talk, but we pontificate. All of us flex the muscles of our influence from time to time. All of us suffer from the transient egoistic erosions of our humility brought on by success. The unfortunate among us are those for whom the erosion is not just a transient one.

Man has always constructed social systems of power. Hierarchies of influence have existed since time immemorial. Political power is always at the peak of any hierarchy.

By definition, a politician is a human manipulator. He must impose his will on others; a consequence of the power inherent in the responsibility of making decisions for others. He is as powerful as he is capable of influencing the lives of his constituents. His prestige is measured by the number of individuals who submit to the decisions he makes.

The demands of political urgency do not usually permit politicians the luxury of achieving changes through time-consuming educative processes. Instead, they turn to persuasion in order to get the people they govern to follow their dictates.

No matter how effectively conceived and executed, any representative government deals with vast accumulations of power. Even in our democratically conceived system of representative government, political power has to corrupt political leaders; there is no way to control all the abuses of influence. In spite of our structure of checks and balances, there are limitations to the extent to which power can police power. Nevertheless, to maintain any society, there must be a group of political leaders who control the power structure. Their positions of power will restrict their capacity for more shared loving. Apparently, we are destined to be governed by those who are more loveless than loving.

Our national success has come at a critical time in human affairs. Modern technology makes it more possible to concentrate power than ever before. Through the mass media we are also more vulnerable to manipulation by those in power than was previously the case. Consequently, it is easier than ever for a powerful few to influence the day-to-day fate of the many.

Our capacity to love is in greater jeopardy today than it has ever been. Our individual narcissism has never been more accessible to provocation from external forces. Indeed, our narcissism is actually being provoked more today than ever before.

Today, living requires great individual strength; greater personal maturity is necessary in order to neutralize the impact of today's manipulative onslaught. It is harder than ever to preserve one's personal integrity; it is more difficult to care about anyone else. Each of us is more victimized by the collective national success.

Success is not an evil quality in itself, but it does

represent a force that stimulates us into moving toward a greater degree of narcissism. Success is not the crippling factor. The narcissism that springs from it is, particularly as expressed through the hunger for power that it creates.

11 /

The Media: Greenhouse for Narcissistic Flowering

If power is a form of narcissistic prostitution, then the media is the world's best brothel for procuring it.

No force influences our lives more profoundly than the media. It forms our view of the world, shapes our perceptions of everything around us, allows us to become familiar with all things. There is little that it cannot show us. Its reach is beyond our comprehension.

The United States has the highest level of media development in the world. No other society has the integrated media resources—newspapers, magazines, radio, and television—that we have. And it is just beginning. What can happen in the future, and no doubt will, is mind-boggling.

Even now it touches every aspect of our lives. It provides us with rudimentary medical education, teaching us about personal health and how to protect it. It explores the ramifications of mental health, offering homespun psychological guidance. It instructs us about the nutritional value of the things we eat and drink, and tells us where to buy them and how to cook them. It brings religion into our homes, placing the pulpit in the middle of our living rooms. It entertains us with everything from Archie Bunker to *Holocaust*. It allows us to be present at the moment man steps foot on the moon, and to witness the collapse of a presidency. It baby-sits for our children at the same time that it distorts their conceptions about life.

The art of mass manipulation has emerged from the development of the media and has grown into a major industry. It is the business of advertising.

Advertising supports the media, and the media supports advertising. Advertisers have succeeded in making their products the nouns of our society, symbols of a whole way of life. Coca-Cola isn't just a drink; it's an American idiom throughout the world. Travelers find security in its presence. "Coke Is Life" is more than a simple slogan.

Coke has no monopoly on the logos that have become symbols of the American way of life throughout the world. Whether it's Mobil's flying horse, Shell's shell, Ford's better idea, Kellogg's tiger, Big Mac's Ronald McDonald, Pepsi's tri-color, or the Kentucky Colonel's shining white countenance, American advertising first homogenized this country, then the world.

The media makes things recognizable; it breeds familiarity. We learn to attach a sense of well-being to all that is familiar. Indeed, the media ultimately addicts us to the familiar. Once a product becomes a household name, it has a guaranteed longevity. Take the label off the Campbell's Soup can and its desirability vanishes. We don't buy the contents, we buy the label. Familiar labels are safe, the unfamiliar risky. The media trains us to believe that. It determines what does and does not become part of our lives.

In time, those who managed the media realized they could sell not only things but also people. So they generated celebrities.

Celebrities have become an integral part of the American way of life. No society in the world is more solicitous of them than we are. We give them too much power, we pay them too much, and we give them too much credence. A popular actor is not the best judge of candidates for elective office. A great athlete is not trained to make judgments about the superiority of medical products.

Celebrity power has spun out of control in this country. The advertising industry has generated pay scales for celebrities that are ludicrous. To pay an actor two million dollars as a guaranteed income for three weeks of work in a movie is ridiculous. To pay a gifted athlete one million dollars for publicly playing his sport makes no sense. To pay a model a fee of two thousand dollars an hour for exhibiting the accidental attributes of her birth is beyond reason. To pay a pop musician two million dollars or more for recording an album borders on social insanity.

I am not suggesting that talented professionals should not be highly paid. But why should the difference between an entertainer's earnings and a professional teacher's, for instance, be so vast? Teachers are surely just as important to the well-being of our society, yet they earn only between fifteen thousand dollars and twenty thousand dollars a year for the vital responsibility of shaping our future by educating our young! And what about the President of the United States, whose overall talents should be second to none?

Such discrepancies in earning power may seem unreasonable, but the point is that the media *is* unreasonable. Reason is not a component of narcissism. In the media, images not only become reality, they can become more meaningful than reality itself. We sell cars with Catherine Deneuve, shaving cream with Farrah Fawcett-Majors, gasoline with Bob Hope, and American Express with Karl Malden. Give a product the right image and it can be sold to anyone whether he needs it or not and with little regard to whether it is good for him or not.

One of the most serious recent extensions of media power occurs in the political process. Men are elected to the highest office in the land based on their media image. Our President—as did several of his recent predecessors—has a makeup man, a wardrobe man, a specially trained speech-writing staff, and even a hairdresser to help him obscure his bald spot. They are the charisma experts. Charisma is marketable, and it is their job to help create it. The image of leadership is the operating rule; it does not necessarily relate to a candidate's actual ability to lead. We sell a President the same way we sell breakfast cereal: through images. Use John Wayne to capture the Republican vote. Use Robert Redford for the ecologists and Paul Newman, Shirley MacLaine, or Jack Nicholson for the liberals. The nation of the people, by the people, and for the people is rapidly becoming a society of the media, by the media, and for the media.

Almost all other countries restrain the proliferation of the media. The form of limitation ranges from totalitarian control through censorship to restrictions of daily programming time in the more democratic and open societies. Nowhere has the media been allowed to increase as profusely as it has in the United States.

Marshall McLuhan must have been writing about us when he issued his predictions about "the wired city." He warned us that the media was a force with its own built-in program of growth, one that would proliferate to the point where it would ultimately control those who naïvely believed they could regulate it. The media's power is apparently so great that the only possible way to contain it may be to shut it down.

The media feeds on those who need it most, including the celebrities it gives birth to. They are permitted to bask in the intense, heady glow of the media limelight only for a while. Then, after being consumed by the media, they are discarded. The list of the "passing parade" grows every day. Not only people are vulnerable, but labels as well. The Guccis, Puccis, St. Laurents, and Cassinis that are "in" today may be "out" tomorrow.

The "Big Brother" potential of the media is feared in most of the world. Its impact is not only psychological but biological. Recent research on brain physiology has introduced new concerns relative to its influence. Marshall McLuhan describes the possibility of reinforcing the control of the left hemisphere of the brain over the right by media programming, which fosters passive receptivity by feeding us all the information we require without any effort on our part. It even goes beyond giving information: it interprets it for us. As a result, the need to develop the more feeling and empathic half of our brain is undermined. McLuhan feels that the media further compromises our society by contributing to the increase of the passive, nonfeeling, rational, uncreative, and unassertive among our citizenry.

The potential for the abuse of power is always present in power itself. That is certainly true of the media.

Mind control is one of the most threatening aspects of contemporary technology. As our skills at human conditioning become more subtle and more efficient, the media provides better and better means for its implementation. The slightest bias in the reporting of the news can reverberate far into the future. The distorted dramatic characterization of a historical figure can change a national tradition.

The media can be used to manipulate us into giving up individual choice in favor of collective conditioning. This will inevitably happen if the media continues to concentrate and accumulate power. Such growth of power will, in turn, increasingly stimulate narcissism. The narcissism that the power proliferates will further serve the power itself. The media is such a narcissistic agent that it reinforces and is reinforced by the innate narcissistic pools in each of us. This sets up a circular chain of events. The media stimulates our narcissism. In turn, the excitement stirred up in our narcissism attracts us to the media, which set it off in the first place. The investment of our heightened narcissism back into the media serves to increase the narcissistic quality of the media itself. This enables the media to trigger a new cycle of narcissistic flow from the media to us and back to the media again; but each new cycle would be at a higher level of narcissistic input than the previous one.

In this fashion, the stature of the media as a narcissistic force can only increase. It is designed to selectively reinforce its own narcissistic prejudice. The more power it accumulates, the more narcissism it generates; the more narcissism it generates, the more narcissism is reflected back to it.

As a result of that constantly revolving circle of events, those who control the media are, by definition, narcissists. The narcissism inherent in the power of the media attracts narcissists in the first place. And in those instances where someone who comes to work for the media is not a primarily narcissistic person to begin with, he will inevitably become one as the media progressively elevates his narcissistic level to the position of primacy in his own makeup. The media sympathetically vibrates with his innate narcissistic forces and thereby enables them to break through. There are no exceptions to this rule. We are all vulnerable.

The media in the United States is the most powerful and pervasive in the world. It is no accident, therefore, that we have come to be regarded as the most narcissistic nation of all. The caricature of the Ugly American is a universal portrait. He is a narcissist—loud, self-centered, and boasting that Americans do everything better than anyone else. He throws his money around to display his wealth and wears the military might of his country as a badge of his own personal greatness.

"We're the richest and strongest, therefore we're the greatest," he says.

The narcissistic focus of our media creates a serious problem. For a free society to remain open, all points of view must be represented. Technically, this is possible. There is no inherent prejudice in the inanimate elements that make the media come to life. Ink, sound waves, and optical waves move in whatever directions they are energized by human beings. It is people who govern the message. In the case of the United States, it is our commitment to a power elite who governs the media that leads it down an increasingly narcissistic path.

In the film industry, for example, there are fewer and fewer motion pictures about human commitment. The hero today is not a moralist with integrity. He is an anti-hero who attacks the establishment as a symbol of oppression rather than as something he can creatively change. He feels it is perfectly all right to use violence in support of his ends. The ends justify the means.

The highest level of such a sentiment is represented by the James Bond syndrome. This character, whom the film industry made an international hero, is clearly a psychopath. Fortunately for us, he is a psychopath on the side of goodness and God. Unfortunately, he fosters in those in his audience, who also feel they are on the side of goodness and God, an imitative conviction that they should be able to enjoy the same narcissistic privileges that he has enjoyed. He is a superstud with a license to use women anywhere and any time he finds them, and is a vigilante of law and order for whom the end always justifies the means. Even murder is applauded.

Films based on the quality of human tenderness are the exception to the rule. In spite of the episodic success of a *Love Story*, studios are more apt to produce a *Dirty Harry, Marathon Man, Black Sunday, The Texas*

Chain Saw Massacre, and other varieties of narcissistic violence.

More and more films display the narcissistic character as an exciting life style—from *Alfie* to *Petulia, Shampoo, Bobby Deerfield,* and so forth. Glib talk, stylish cars trimmed to appear individualistic, fleeting relationships with beautiful people, and great wealth and the incredible influence associated with it fill our entertainment packages. *The Greek Tycoon* was constructed around real tragedy plus a yacht with hot and cold running women and an electric hull that opened so that the characters could jump directly from bed to water. *The Other Side of Midnight* made the private plane a household utensil and sexual revenge an admirable motive.

Caring is too often portrayed as weakness. People are expendable. The caring hero is obsolete. So is the caring heroine. Today's hero is a macho figure: cool, aloof, and invulnerable. Today's heroine is "liberated": cool, aloof, and aggressive. Commitments to other human beings are intrusive because they limit the ability to compete.

The quality of the product produced by the media reflects the quality of personal commitment among the vast majority of people who work in that arena. The power game there is so intense that it requires most of one's energy to remain viable in the competition. When you work in the public eye, there is no such thing as a status quo. Either you keep moving up or you fail.

Failure in the media has a quality unique unto itself. It is more than being bruised. It means being isolated and ignored. In most walks of life, people who become depressed subsequent to a failure overreact and often feel it is the end of the world. But the world goes right on and they usually recover and get back into it. Not so in the media. Failure can indeed mean the end of the world. Once you've fallen from grace in the media, there are no more "social" overtures from colleagues, no more invitations to industry screenings, no more telephone calls, no more of much of anything. Your name is usually removed from your assigned parking space before you even get to your car. The wipeout is total. The higher the stakes, the bigger the risks. And there is no greater risk for a narcissist than public humiliation. In the media no one is humiliated in private.

The narcissistic perspective is ingrained throughout all the media. It is not confined to television, print, or radio. In the legitimate theater, for example, plays are more often than not depressing experiences. The themes acted out on our contemporary stages are most usually "down" ones. Escapism seems to have escaped.

Today, many of our playwrights offer their own special brand of reality. It is a narcissistic view of man that takes him apart and dramatizes his human failings. Unfortunately, all too often our leading playwrights fail to put man back together again after they have dissected him. Consequently, the playgoing experience frequently leaves us feeling less than we were instead of more for having attended the theater. We are left with little hope. Play after play points out that man cannot love—he is too self-centered, too narcissistic.

Does the media stimulate new behavior or does it reflect existing patterns of behavior? This is the raging issue among media leaders and critics alike. Media leaders protect themselves by defending the media as a reflection of society. Media critics, and a growing body of scholars, attack the media as a force that undermines society by stimulating new behavior. In my judgment, it does both. It sets a new pace as well as keeps up the paces already established. It can lead to establishing new values, new interests, and new attitudes.

Successful media events lead to a multitude of related happenings and products. Consequently, every major film studio now has a merchandising division. *Star Wars* is more than a successful film; it is a marketing complex of toys, games, clothes, music, posters, advertising royalties, books, and discos. The *Annie Hall* look is now visible in an entire range of women's apparel. *Saturday Night Fever*, itself an enormously successful film, made the hustle a national craze and may earn far more in music royalties than it will as a film.

The media influences the words we use, the clothes we wear, the places we visit, the interests we pursue, even the kinds of people we admire. The media is far more than a reflection of society. Its role and influence are vital to our future, particularly when one recognizes that the media is dominated by the narcissistic point of view.

In an open society the ultimate control over the abuse of power lies in the collective majority. If we continue to let only narcissistic leaders dominate the media, we forfeit our responsibility. We will deprive ourselves of the opportunity to experience opposing points of view, fresh perspectives, and new visions related to more shared loving values instead of narcissistic values. Sex and violence sell, so we are inundated with these elements. Tenderness doesn't sell, so we're given only a token amount to assuage those who know we should have more.

All of this at a time when the media is on the verge of an almost inconceivable proliferation. It will make everything that has come before minuscule by comparison. Controlling the networks will be like child's play compared with the outcome of the contest over who will control the satellites.

By controlling the satellites, one society can inflict its ideology upon another; one country can undermine the basic beliefs of another. Israel's interest in increasing its population can play havoc with India's desperate need to limit its own. The absence of religion in Russia's Marxist society can have a devastating effect on a Catholic nation such as Spain. Attitudes about personal liberties in the United States can be terribly disruptive in the Philippines.

Who is to say that one nation has the right to impose its values on another? Who controls the airspace that surrounds the earth? Who monitors the light and sound waves? Who studies the messages they carry? Who designates appropriate territories for transmission and reception? Who designates the right of some of us to control what belongs to all of us? Who ensures that what belongs to all of us is not used only by a few of us, and only then to harm the rest of us?

Any stone dropped into the huge ocean of the media generates waves that will pound into infinity. Throughout the ages people have appeared who sought to dominate the entire world—from Genghis Khan to Adolph Hitler. They failed. But they tried to do it the hard way, one territory at a time. The first tyrant to master the media may succeed where others have failed.

The media can serve us or it can rape us. The choice is ours to make. If we demand the expression of more loving values, we can control the growing narcissistic infestation spread by the media. If we don't make that demand, the narcissistic infestation will not only continue, it will grow and overcome us all.

12 /

Violence:
The Wake of Narcissism

Hell hath no fury like a narcissist scorned. Yet for a narcissist, being scorned is inevitable. In fact, the more narcissistic one is, the greater the potential for being scorned because of the greater demands for gratification. The greater the demands for gratification, the greater the chance of frustration. To a narcissist, frustration is being scorned by the society he expects to feed him and take care of all his needs.

The narcissist places great demands on society. He wants so much that he is always in a state of unfulfillment. He is always in a state of irritability because narcissism is insatiable. He is always reaching out for more, and more is never enough. There is never too much adulation, sexual gratification, material possessions, prestige, and power.

He creates constant pressure on the people around him, who are driven to protect themselves from being overwhelmed by the relentless barrage of his demands. This, in turn, sets off feelings of guilt within the loving people who relate to him, because of their inability to supply his endless needs.

Social scientists have always associated aggression with frustration. The greater the frustration, the greater the aggression. Since frustration is an inevitable part of living, all of us experience some feelings of aggression in our daily lives.

Part of the process of moving from a self-centered, narcissistic infant to a social animal capable of loving requires learning to tolerate frustration. The frustration of a child by his parents is the primary means through which he is taught to redirect his narcissism. The more his narcissism persists, the greater will be his resistance to frustration.

Aggression does not necessarily lead to violence. Violence is a special form of behavior in which aggressive feelings are directly expressed toward other human beings who are either real or symbolic representations of the source of his frustration. One resorts to violence only when all other means of dealing with frustration fail. It is not regarded as an acceptable problem-solving method, but as an irrational act caused by an inability to manage frustration.

Why, then, has violence become a common problem-solving means in our society? Why has the expression of violence erupted? Why does the number of violent acts increase each and every year? Why is it utilized as the problem-solving method of choice by more and more of us? Has our ability to manage frustration decreased, or is it that there is so much more of it now? One thing is certain: violence is more a part of our everyday lives than ever before.

The United States is regarded as the most violent country in the world. And not only are we the leader in that regard, but our lead increases every year.

There are approximately twenty thousand criminal homicides a year in the United States, a rate of about eight murders per a population of one hundred thousand. The chance of an individual's death from homicide is greater than the likelihood of his dying from many of the major diseases. And this probability is growing. The rate of criminal homicide is climbing about eight percent per year. These statistics do not account for all killings—they do not include the undetected homicides, those carried out in the line of duty by law-enforcement personnel, and other "justifiable" forms of murder.

There was a time when murder was not part of our everyday life. Thirty years ago, even the thought of the possibility that an acquaintance could be murdered was totally alien to most of us. Today, unfortunately, not one of us would be shocked beyond comprehension should a friend or even a member of one's family be murdered. Indeed, if we search our reservoir of friends and acquaintances, most of us already know at least one person who has been brutally attacked or murdered.

Homicide is not the only form of violent behavior to increase. There are approximately 750,000 violent crimes annually. And these are only the reported violent crimes. We are all rapidly becoming candidates for this type of crime.

Some of the most violent crimes are committed by children. Juvenile gangs are one of the most complex law-enforcement problems of today. They commit the entire range of violent crimes: burglary, mugging, rape, and murder. Their youth protects them from strong legal prosecution. Consequently, they are soon free to repeat their criminal behavior.

Why so much crime among children today? We have always been aware that children are capable of greater cruelty than adults. This reflects the greater degree of narcissism that is normally present in all children. They are more emotionally immature and have not yet adequately incorporated the social consciousness of their elders. But why are they becoming increasingly violent? Are they even more narcissistic than those who preceded them? Is this an indication of what is yet to come?

Violence is not restricted to our streets and schools. It has invaded our homes—child abuse, spouse beating, sexual assault, and sibling violence. Over one million children from age three to seventeen have parents who have attacked them at least once with a lethal weapon. Almost two million wives are beaten by their husbands annually, usually twice. Well over two million children have used a knife or a gun on a brother or a sister. About ten percent of the annual criminal homicides in this country involve husbands and wives.

It is difficult to communicate through statistics. They are too impersonal. They always seem to deal with the other fellow and not with us. It is all too easy to get lost in the collective crowd and hide from any personal impact. Yet it is impossible to deny the reality of these numbers dealing with violence. There is no place left to hide. It is no longer the other fellow. It is us.

One of the reasons why violence today affects us all is because of the change in its quality. In the past, we could find security in the knowledge that we had done nothing to warrant a violent attack from anyone else. We felt safe because violence was an act motivated by some specific issue of contention between people. If no serious conflict existed between ourselves and anyone else, we had every right to feel safe.

Such is no longer the case. Now most violence is gratuitous. If you're in the wrong place at the wrong time, you're it. Violence has nothing to do with you personally; it is provoked only by your accidental presence. There is no safety anywhere. As we walk down any street, approaching footsteps make us anxious. Driving on a highway or walking across a campus, we can become the victim of a sniper. We can be mugged anywhere, any time, by any addict who needs anybody's money for a fix. All unfamiliar places and people are seen as potential sources of danger. Even the familiar is not without some threat.

The most serious aspect of gratuitous violence is the way it has become ingrained in our society. The victim becomes as much a part of the act as the criminal. By living with the expectation of violence, we implicitly accept the reality that it will be inherent in our lives. This acceptance serves to breed violence. The expectant attitude communicates directly to the criminal our readiness for a violent act to occur.

The extent to which violence has been ingrained in our daily lives is indicated by the ground rules—reported in one of our national magazines—for walking the streets of New York City. There is a fee for safe passage. You can buy immunity from physical harm when confronted by a mugger if you carry at least $150 in your pocket.

We no longer believe that our police can protect us. There are too few of them and far too many criminals. We are also convinced that no one will rise to our defense if we are attacked. It's too dangerous. So each of us walks alone through a maze of anticipated violence.

The burglar-alarm industry is reaping the profits of our justified paranoia. At the rate these alarms are being installed, soon no home will be complete without one.

The sale of handguns is increasing dramatically. We say we need them for protection. There are presently forty million of them in the hands of the American public. Two and a half million are sold every year. A handgun is bought every thirteen seconds, and someone is killed by one every forty-eight minutes. Since we can't count on the police to protect us, we decide we must protect ourselves. We depend less and less on the social institutions of law and order. It's every man for himself.

Violence need not only be directed toward someone else; it can be directed at one's self. The only difference between homicide and suicide is the direction in which the gun is aimed. Both acts require murderous intent.

The suicide rate in the United States has increased

tremendously. It has grown from 10.6 suicides per 100,000 population in 1960 to 27.1 suicides per 100,000 population in 1975. Most dramatically, it has increased among adolescents. The rate of suicide among the young is three hundred to four hundred percent greater than it was two decades ago. Today it is unusual for an adolescent to emerge into adult life without knowing someone in his circle of friends who has made a suicidal gesture, if not actually committed suicide.

Why has all hell broken loose? Why are we impotent to control violence? Why do we accept it as part of our way of life?

There are many theories that attempt to explain the growth of violence. They agree on some things, differ on others. Yet they are unanimous in recognizing that violence is increasingly a problem-solving alternative in our culture. There is less and less room for respected differences of opinion between people in conflict.

The solution of choice today seems to require doing the other person in, literally or symbolically. If you don't agree with a man's politics, you can always kill him, whether that man is President of the United States or a local candidate for dog catcher. If you don't like the color of a man's skin, you can always burn down his house. If you're a have-not, you can attack the haves as a statement of your resentment and your feelings of being entitled to a fairer share. On the other hand, if you're a have person, you can persecute the have-nots in order to control their sense of rage at being deprived.

It has never been possible to police an entire society directly. However, it was never meant to be possible. Ultimately, a society can be effectively policed only from within by the individual compliance of its citizens, not exclusively from without by an externally imposed police force. Policemen are meant to represent symbols of the need for individual self-discipline through compliance with the law.

All of us are familiar with the effect of the presence of a police car on the way we drive. In those instances, even when we are moving well within the prescribed speed limits, we tend to slow down. The mere sight of the patrol car serves as a stimulus that almost automatically compels us to look at our speedometer and check the speed at which we are driving. It symbolizes our need to police ourselves.

Loving human beings live with a feeling of obligation to others. This is the essence of social consciousness. It is experienced through feelings of guilt when we do not adequately consider the interests of others while acting upon our own interests. The narcissism that is present in all of us motivates each of us, in some measure, to behave in uncaring ways. Loving people, therefore, always live with some degree of guilt by virtue of being in conflict with their narcissistic self-interests. That guilt polices their behavior.

Narcissistic people, on the other hand, are so self-centered they do not experience guilt sufficiently to police their behavior. Their self-appointed right to be special frees them from the need to concern themselves about the rights of others. Such narcissistic people are the ones who need to be policed the most, because they have the greatest potential for violence. They are the most likely to express rage as a consequence of frustration and the least willing to police themselves.

In one form or another, every social situation symbolizes the original society of the family. Societies can exist only by appealing to the loving qualities learned within our families during early childhood. A majority of citizens must retain these loving qualities for a society to continue to function.

In and of itself, society cannot make us care. It is totally dependent on the existence of the learned capacity for more shared loving among the majority of its citizens in order to survive. This is an absolutely essential prerequisite. It cannot be waived, nor is there any way around it. Unless enough people care, a society cannot continue to exist.

It is easy to police the behavior of loving people. All a society needs to do is symbolically trigger the feelings of guilt that serve to control them.

In the absence of a well-entrenched sense of conscience, symbolic enforcement fails. Only literal enforcement—policing each of us on an individual basis —will work. But obviously, no society can afford the cost, either in money or in personnel, of placing enough police on the street to achieve such literal enforcement.

A growing need to increase the size of police forces is a signal that a society is failing. It means that an increasing amount of citizens no longer feel adequate guilt when relating to their fellow man. It indicates a shift within the population from loving to narcissism.

Society is an artificial, man-made structure designed to circumvent the law of nature, which permits only the most fit to survive. In the absence of society we return to our primitive ways. Life once again becomes a kill-or-be-killed proposition.

The rampant violence pervading this country is a sure indication that our society is failing.

A growing number of politicians are loudly campaigning with promises of enlarging our law enforcement agencies. They seek to put more police in the streets. Some also seek to restore capital punishment, require mandatory prison sentences, subject juveniles to stricter criminal prosecution, and crack down on what they call a system of justice that is too soft. Such efforts are probably doomed to fail. An entire society can not be literally policed. Ultimately violence must be controlled from within, not from without.

We are violent because we no longer love enough.

We no longer care enough about our fellow man to be concerned about his well-being. We are too concerned for ourselves. There is too much greed, too much hoarding, too much wanting. Most significant of all, we have become collectively too narcissistic.

The narcissist is a violent man. He is always trying to get as much as he can, even if it is more than he is entitled to. He uses his power to manipulate others and make them subservient to him. He is not encumbered by a sense of justice. He believes he is entitled to whatever he can get. He is the killer of our society.

Our violence is an unequivocal symptom of the decline of the United States as a socially viable country. We will never be able to neutralize the incredible proliferation of our rage by merely providing more policemen. There will never be enough burglar alarms to protect us from violent intrusions. There will never be enough handguns to defend ourselves.

The solution to violence can come about only by re-creating our sense of responsibility for our fellow man. This can be achieved only by employing the feelings of guilt that caring people are capable of having. It is the price for social living.

There is violence in all of us because there is narcissism in all of us. The more narcissistic we are, the more violent we will be. We have already reached a level of violence where living is constantly crowded by fear. Have we reached the point of no return? It is impossible to know. But one thing is certain. We're pretty far down the road. We can't afford to let this go on any longer. We will either move away from the self-centeredness of narcissism or perish violently.

13 /

Education: A Myth of Reason

How can we perpetuate our capacity for loving? How can we have enough narcissistic spice in our lives to enrich them without losing our ability to care? How can we protect the enduring pleasure we get through loving from the relentless pressures of our persistent narcissistic hungers?

Can we police our universal vulnerabilities through education? Beginning with the classrooms of our childhood, can we be taught to make narcissism work for us instead of becoming enslaved by it?

Man has taught himself to change his existence dramatically. The changes, however, relate almost exclusively to the application of his intellectual capabilities. Human existence has altered to the extent that we now live in a world where the essentials for survival are readily available. Food, water, and shelter against the elements—both natural and man-made—have been integrated into our society. Through a deeper understanding of the laws governing natural phenomena, we have organized scientific disciplines that enable us to build an ever-expanding human technology. We no longer hunt; we go to the grocery store. We no longer search for water; we turn on our tap. We no longer move from cave to cave for refuge from the perils of nature; we lodge ourselves in apartments and homes.

We have learned to overcome our natural isolation, first with gestures and grunts, then by signs scrawled on cave walls, and finally with language. Language has enabled us to systematize communication with one another.

Mass transportation makes it possible for us to travel anywhere on earth. Our geographic isolation has vanished; it gave way first to the occasional explorer and then to the regularly scheduled arrivals of supersonic aircraft. There are no places left for primitive societies to hide. Our world is moving closer and closer to becoming a conglomerate mass. Our individual fate is becoming inextricably linked to the fate of all mankind.

Yet, in spite of these profound and almost unbelievable changes, there is no evidence that we are emotionally different from our prehistoric ancestors. Our struggles are different in external form but not in basic quality. We are still searching for more enduring happiness and for the kind of pleasure that we can sustain throughout our lives.

We have increased our probabilities for survival and vastly improved our physical comforts during life on earth. But we continue to be plagued by fear. Indeed, our fear is more pervasive than it has ever been before. As our external security increases, so does our fear. It has changed only in its character.

The meaning of survival has changed; it has shifted from a physical struggle to exist to a need to find purpose and meaning in life. Our daily lives continue to be filled with greed, envy, violent competition, and uncontrollable hoarding—maybe to an even greater extent than ever.

In contrast to man's intellectual achievements, his humanistic qualities have not grown at all. In relative terms, they have declined. There are more people to share with, yet he shares less. Each of us strives to accumulate material reservoirs far in excess of any practical potential for their utilization. The waste from the haves is greater than the needs of the have-nots.

It is difficult to reconcile the difference between our intellectual advances and our emotional development. The widening gap between our ability to care and our ability to reason is inescapable. Is the lag an inherent quality of human nature or the result of our incompetence at educating ourselves?

One of the unique qualities of the American way of life has been—and still is—our commitment to public education. Anyone who wants an education can have it. The educational opportunities available in this country are unequaled anywhere else in the world. Our national investment in education has not been without merit. It has produced the fantastic technology that is now part of our everyday life and that has contributed to making us the greatest industrial nation in the history of mankind. One has only to recall the image of man on the moon to understand the stature of our scientific sophistication.

Technology, however, is limited with regard to the extent that it contributes to our lives. It cannot help us to be able to love more. It increases the dimensions of our world, but not the potential for social survival. It has proved to be far more proficient, both in increasing our facilities for manipulating one another and in providing complicated weaponry for destroying one another, than it has in enhancing our commitment to coexistence. Technology does not endure; it always leads to its own obsolescence. Every new invention contains within it the precursor of its replacement. As we develop an anti-ballistic missile system, we simultaneously anticipate its neutralization by an anti-anti-ballistic missile system. Only the human being is irreplaceable.

Technology is a direct extension of our intellect. It

reflects the degree to which our intelligence is responsive to training. The appeal of our intellect to order and reason makes it the ideal avenue for learning. Indeed, our educational systems are built around our intellectual capacities.

The primacy of intelligence in structuring our educational systems is not a consequence of free choice; it is a matter of default. We have no other alternative. The irrational aspect of man is far more difficult to reach. It does not pursue logical order and it defies reason. It is not accessible and, therefore, not readily trainable.

Nevertheless, man's irrational core is critical to his fate. This irrational core is made up of his innate biological urges and desires. It is the home of his narcissism. To reach his narcissism—and thereby help him understand and control it—a whole new educational process is essential. Without it, the lag between man's reasonable and unreasonable dimensions will continue to grow, eventually reaching a point that will be beyond repair.

Dewey and James directed us to educate the "whole man," not just his mind. This idea rapidly became an educational slogan. No teacher passed muster who did not commit himself to this goal. It is rather like being against sin and devoted to truth. But it is easier said than done. We just don't know how to do it. Try as we may with an endless stream of progressive innovations—child-centered classrooms, motivation through need, heterogenous and homogenous groupings, the new math—we fail every time. We don't know how to teach people to love through formal classroom education.

In our intellectually preoccupied educational system, the intelligence quotient has emerged as the yardstick by which the curriculum is evaluated. We're not even sure what the intelligence quotient really measures, and yet we have made it the cornerstone of our educational process.

By definition, bright students are those with high IQ's. In our schools, therefore, they are expected to get high grades. When enough of them do not, we assume that the teaching program is ineffective. So we make changes in the teaching based on the assumption that something is wrong.

The effectiveness of those changes is then determined by the subsequent performance of the same bright-student group. If the high-IQ students do well, we are satisfied that we have corrected the problem; if they do not do well, we continue to change the program until they do. It is a closed system; one in which IQ is used to predict school performance at the same time that it is used as the means of guaranteeing the very performance it predicts.

We don't have simple numbers to designate the more narcissistic from the less narcissistic, the more rage-filled from the less rage-filled, the more tender from the less tender, the gentle from the tough. We cannot quantify our ability to feel, care, and share into a mechanical measurement. Even if we could, from a teaching point of view, we wouldn't know what to do with it. At present, it cannot realistically be dealt with in the confines of a classroom. Intelligence is much easier for us to work with. So our schools take the easier way. They defer to what they can do instead of working to change what we must change.

If anything, over the years we have increased our worship at the shrine of intellect. The ranks of standardized objective tests swell with each passing day. They increase not only in number but also in importance. More and more of our educational structures are being built around test scores. Scholastic Aptitude Tests, Law Aptitude Tests, Medical Aptitude Tests, aptitude tests for everything. Each is produced on demand by a small body of "exalted men" sitting in their ivy-covered towers, arrogant enough to believe they can predict who will make the better doctors, the better lawyers, the better students.

Is the better lawyer the man who will be more clever at concealment in drafting a contract or more equitable? Is the better doctor more knowledgeable or more dedicated to healing? Is the better student the more proficient academic achiever or the more humanistic? Not only do the aptitude test-makers know which one is better, they have a quick and efficient method for picking him out in advance.

Aptitude testing is an effective means of giving those children whose prior school performance was poor a chance to obtain an education that might otherwise be denied to them. It grows out of our understanding of underachievement; children whose work was undermined by a disabling circumstance such as a physical or an emotional difficulty are given an opportunity to redefine their potential.

Aptitude testing has a distinct place in our educational system, but unfortunately, it provides such a nice, neat number by which students can be judged that it has become all-pervasive. The tail is now wagging the dog. Underachievers no longer constitute a special minority who deserve another chance; their interests have been misdirected by our misguided educators and dominate those of the majority.

Countless examples of the abuse of aptitude-test scores exist in every instance of scholastic admission practices. Take the case of an emotionally well-adjusted young man who had set out to pursue a career in medicine. He was a sensitive, gentle person with a deep interest in helping others. He was of above-average intelligence but not superior, as recorded by his IQ.

He came from a family with a modest income, and it was necessary for him to work while attending high school. He was a fine athlete, but his after-school employment made it impossible for him to play on his school team. He achieved a B+ average in his studies but won no special awards. He did, however, have very good college recommendations from a number of his teachers.

The financial resources of his family did not make it possible for him to live away from home while attending college. So he enrolled at a university that was located in his home town. He continued to work during vacations and after his classes in order to contribute to his tuition.

From the very beginning of his college education, he was aware that it would be difficult to obtain admission to medical school. His interest in studying medicine, however, was so strong that he was determined to qualify. He worked very hard and obtained a B+ average. In addition, his candidacy for medical school was strongly supported by professors who were impressed with his humanity and his diligence.

In applying to medical school, he was required to take a medical aptitude examination. He did, and on repeated occasions scored poorly. Consequently, he was rejected by each of the eleven schools to which he had applied.

At the same time a friend and classmate of his also applied to study medicine. While attending college, that friend could not discipline himself to work at his studies. His interest in medicine was marginal; in applying, he was responding primarily to pressure from his father, who was a physician. He was able to achieve only a B— average and could not get good recommendations. But, unlike his classmate, when this young man took the medical aptitude test, he scored very highly. Consequently, he succeeded in being admitted to three of the eleven medical schools from which his friend was rejected.

It took a lot of conviction by admissions officers of the medical schools to reject a boy who had performed well over a sustained period of four years in favor of another candidate who performed well over a sustained period of about eight hours. But such is the nature of the convictions of admissions officers these days. They have permitted themselves to believe that a single test designed by a group of mortal men can better identify the potentially more competent physician than four long years of proven performance. I do not object to using an aptitude test score to give an underachiever a second chance. But I do object when it is done at the expense of someone whose performance is better in every way except on his aptitude test score.

The incredible rise in the cost of medical care has been accompanied by the exposure of abuses of programs like Medicare. We also encounter in the press every day accounts of physicians who have exploited their right to prescribe medicine by profiting from drug abuse. It appears, therefore, that medical aptitude tests have not succeeded in screening out the uncaring and unethical physician. We seem to need other means to identify those students for whom the Hippocratic oath will be more than a graduation ritual.

The quality of our attorneys leaves something to be desired as well. In the recent past, Watergate led to a broad criticism of the legal profession. The abuses by lawyers—the guardians of our society—were exposed.

Law schools base their selection of candidates on intellectual performance as measured by grades and aptitude scores, but this technique has failed to ensure the admission of only those who are best qualified because it does not differentiate between those who will commit themselves to protect the humanistic dimensions of the law and those who will not. We have not succeeded in distinguishing the student who will earn his livelihood by maintaining the letter of the law while destroying its spirit from the student who will not violate the spirit of the law.

Our intellectually oriented educational system has produced technology that no longer permits mankind any margin for error. Yet the nature of the human condition is such that man does not function without some room for errors. Mistakes have always been a part of our history; fortunately in the past, the mistakes may have been crippling but were not fatal to the human race. That is no longer the case; today the fate of the entire human race is in peril at all times. The prospect of total self-destruction is always imminent because of the potential for the irrational use of nuclear energy that man has rationally developed.

Enough technological expertise already exists for us to afford to have a moratorium on any new additions for as much as fifty or one hundred years. This would give us time to try to close some of the gap between our caring and uncaring selves. It would enable us to shift from our pragmatic interest in intellect to the challenge of exposing the irrational side of man to the learning process. Man managed to get along before our sophisticated technology existed, so he certainly ought to be able to manage if nothing were added to what already exists.

Suggesting that one halt "the wheels of progress" is never a popular position to take. Indeed, it is usually regarded as sacrilegious; it goes against the very nature of man. That may be true, but one first has to decide what constitutes progress. Is it the proliferation of more and more technology, or is it more loving between man and his fellow man?

During a period of moratorium we could better invest our energies in striving to provide to greater numbers of people those existing products of progress that are now available only to some of us. Or we could learn to use what we already have more efficiently and with less waste—of our food and energy supplies—for instance.

To maintain human life on earth, we all must learn

to share. Not as an altruistic gesture, but as a commitment to collective survival. Human inequities have always existed. There have always been the deprived. But feelings of deprivation have never been as rampant as they are today. The media has taught the less fortunate just how unfortunate they are. It shows us, over and over again, the differences between the haves and the have-nots. It has polarized the world as nothing has before it. It has created a climate of increased interpersonal hostility throughout the universe by constantly exposing us to those things some of us do not have and others of us abuse.

The people in the two-thirds of the world, where life lasts for an average of about thirty-five years, have difficulty in accepting those who resent aging because they can look forward to a life span of seventy-five years. The people in the two-thirds of the world who are starving would find it virtually impossible to comprehend the behavior of those who waste more than we eat.

All behavior has personal meaning. The notion of altruism is just that, a notion. No action is devoid of the desire for some personal return. That is not just how it is; it is how it should be. We share not only for the benefit of others but for our own sake as well. If sharing reduces the levels of tension in the world, it also increases our own chances for survival.

Loving makes sharing possible, but narcissism gets in the way. As in the case of sharing, however, loving is never "pure"; it never exists devoid of some self-interest. Such an unrealistic image of love would destroy the potential for its real existence; it requires of man that he go beyond his own dimensions and ignore his basic nature, which is anchored in narcissism.

There was a time when learning to love was viewed as a luxury meant to enrich the lives of a special few. Most of mankind was too busy learning to survive.

Today learning to develop the capacity for a more

sharing love is in no way a luxury. We need to be able to share if we seek to survive. We need to be able to love in order to share.

Therein lies the challenge to education. To teach us to feel more, rather than only know more. To teach us to care more, rather than only understand more.

14 /

The Human Survival Kit: Feelings

The task of dealing with man's irrational being is the single most important challenge facing us. We must find the ways and means to do it.

At present, in spite of the critical importance to our fate of feeling more sharing love, we don't know how to teach it. There are no applicable classroom techniques, no pools of competent teachers, and no acceptable teacher-training institutions that deal specifically with training the irrational side of man.

Feelings are the key to our irrational core. They provide the signals that inform us about the state of our inner face at any given moment. They can be subtle and difficult to perceive or overpowering to the point of drowning out the awareness of anything else. Feelings make man different from any other animal. They also serve to separate us from one another. Some of us are more capable of expressing them than others. But we all have them.

Feelings emerge only from within. They can be provoked by outside forces but cannot be produced externally. They can be imitated, however, without being actually experienced. Such imitation is called acting.

We all do some of that sometimes, but some of us do a lot of it most of the time.

The more we live with our real feelings, the less we have to live with the imitations. Some people—the actors among us—can fake feelings so well they are hard to distinguish from real ones. Some of the greatest actors in the world have never performed professionally, preferring to commit their acting to their everyday lives.

No matter how good an actor one is, however, he cannot actually feel a feeling unless it truly exists. Our pretensions can deceive others, but not ourselves. The fabric of our feelings comes from our inner face; imitations of feelings, expressed through acting, come from the outer face.

The awareness that feelings are lodged in our inner world has led to the development of the "method acting" technique. Teachers of acting recognized that real feelings are the best model for imitative ones. Therefore, actors are educated to relate situations contained within the contents of a dramatic sequence to experiences in their own lives that evoked feelings similar to those called for in a scene. By thus capturing a feeling from his own life, the actor has the substance around which he can construct his performance; it is the feeling that is central to his acting. Actors have learned to recognize that words alone are not enough; feelings must be communicated in order to reach an audience.

We do not trust others when they do not feel what they are saying. We are consciously or unconsciously searching for someone's feelings to help us evaluate the honesty of his communications to us. Words can be easily adapted to fit our purposes. As a means of self-expression, they can be sincere or insincere; they can be readily distorted, particularly by the more glib among us. Feelings, however, cannot be shaped; they can be faked but not actually constructed in reality. That is what makes them so trustworthy. They reflect our inner faces and, therefore, reveal a part of us that is too deeply ingrained in what we innately are to be fabricated.

All of us have been in situations where a friend expresses "sincere" regrets about a disappointment in our lives. The sincerity of his expressed sympathy is sometimes hard for us to accept. In too many instances, in spite of his professed concerns for us, we detect nothing in the way of true feelings emanating from him. Or, even worse, we do detect his feelings, but they may be of gladness rather than of sorrow; his competitive envy makes him happy that something has not worked out for us, because it satisfies his jealousy about what we might have that he does not.

Feelings are always authentic indicators of an individual's state because they cannot be shaped by will. One cannot feel the way he wants to feel, but only the way he does feel. Feelings can be disguised, however, not only in the way we express them to others, but in the way we experience our own feelings ourselves.

It is not uncommon for someone who is depressed to distort the awareness of his sadness with a veneer of heightened excitement. For example, someone who is feeling down could try to deny it by pushing himself in an exaggerated way to have a good time. He forces his laughter, quickens his pace, and may even indulge himself more than usual. But the artificiality of his forced behavior betrays his true feelings. He laughs too loudly, announces his joy too vociferously, dances too wildly, drinks too much, or takes too many drugs. He doesn't want to face what he is really feeling, so he tries to drown it out by "having a good time."

Feelings cannot be eliminated simply because we don't want them to exist; making believe they aren't there doesn't make them go away. Ultimately, in one form or other, feelings will be expressed. The choice we have is whether we want to face them and deal with them directly, or whether we want to suppress them and leave them to deal with us. If we face our feelings, we give ourselves the opportunity to examine the reason why they exist and to do something about it. If we don't face them, the conditions that produce them are allowed to persist and are free to re-create unwanted feelings again. We are denying ourselves choice, giving up a chance to assume more control over our lives.

When feelings are not dealt with overtly, they are handled internally by the body. They can affect our blood pressure, the activity of our digestive system, our breathing, muscle tone, and thought processes; for that matter, they can affect any and every part of us. If we back away often enough from dealing directly with them, they will exact a great toll from our physical well-being.

The newborn infant has no reluctance to expose his feelings. At birth, there is no outer face to distort the expressions of his inner world. He is free to cry, coo, defecate, move his arms and legs, sleep, and regurgitate whenever he feels the urge to do so. In other words, we all start out "going wherever the feeling takes us."

So how do we get sidetracked along the way? Why do we lose the ability to act as we feel?

By expressing his feelings freely, the child is soon in conflict with his outer world. His family doesn't want him to cry; it disturbs them. On the other hand, they want him to coo and smile in response to them rather than to his inner urges. They don't want him to eliminate or suck whenever he feels like it; they toilet-train him and pull his thumb out of his mouth. They teach him to "control his feelings," but he can't, so he begins to hide them.

It is not long before more of our feelings are suppressed than are expressed. We learn our lessons too well. Recognizing that feelings make us vulnerable, we defend ourselves against vulnerability by avoiding the source. But feelings can't really be avoided, so our system is an ineffective one. We are merely electing to pay internally, prices that could be paid far more cheaply externally. We have little choice about how our body handles feelings; we have a great deal of choice about how the totality of our person can handle a feeling.

If I am sexually excited by an attractive woman, I feel desire for her. I can attempt to make her acquaintance. If she complies and shares my desires, then things will go as I hoped. If she rejects me, I will be bruised, but all is not lost. I can masturbate while enjoying the fantasy that she really wanted me as her lover and can create mental images of our lovemaking. I can also deal with the rejection by displacing my sexual attraction onto some other woman who will have me, and utilize fantasies about the attractive lady who turned me down to enrich the experience.

If I ignore my sexual attraction in the first place, then things will be very different. My sexual excitement will be experienced as irritability, and I can be unpleasant to the same woman I really prefer to seduce. My interest in the woman may also serve to set off an anticipation of rejection; it can be expressed as a feeling of dissatisfaction toward other women who are totally innocent of my misadventure. I can even go to the furthest extreme and deny my sexuality almost completely. I can turn to a life of amoral morality and attack sex in the broadest possible terms.

In choosing to ignore feelings, we deny the essence of what we are; in protecting ourselves from the vulnerability that accompanies feelings, we compromise our own sense of being. We opt for safety over pleasure, living to survive rather than surviving to live.

In the human makeup, feelings are primary, thought is secondary. Thought always reflects feelings, but feelings can exist independent of thought.

In the course of our daily lives we can suppress feelings from conscious awareness or distort their quality when they are a part of our consciousness. In both instances, however, the feelings are still a part of our thinking process; evidence of their presence lies in the very act of suppression and distortion. Something must first exist before it can be distorted or suppressed.

There are always traces of our feelings within us, even when we do not permit ourselves to be conscious of them. Those traces, like the feelings themselves, are the basic data sought by the psychiatrist in his efforts to expose us to ourselves. Because it is the feeling that truly sets the tone of our existence, it is the feeling that must be revealed and dealt with, if we are to help ourselves.

If we are satisfied to live only with our outer faces, we need not know our own feelings. If we want to live more fully and experience our inner selves as well, we must always search for our feelings. Moreover, we must allow ourselves to be what we feel.

There are an increasing number of people who are not what they feel. They act "as if" they feel, but that is as far as they go. When such behavior governs their lives excessively, they become what psychiatrists call "as if" characters. This is meant to identify the person who lives "as if" he were someone else, rather than permitting himself to be himself. Constantly denying and distorting his own feelings, he adopts behavioral façades to present himself as he would like to be seen. The façades change like the coming attractions in a movie theater. He models himself after whatever suits his fancy at a given time. If it's "in" to be sympathetic to the cause of the American Indian, then he's in sympathy. If, on the other hand, conservative postures become more popular, whether he feels it or not, he's just as easily disinterested or antagonistic to the Indian's cause.

The "as if" character constantly positions himself to avoid rejection. For him, rejection is too painful. His narcissism and his dependency require that he win the love of others; the need is so great that he cannot tolerate disaffection or disinterest. So he is driven to become one of our unsung thespians; an actor capable of masking his own feelings through a charade designed to manipulate others to service his narcissistic requirements. Such acting skills are absolutely essential in order to master the "as if" life style.

Caring is possible only through feeling; but in order to allow one's self to feel, one must first have developed the capacity to deal with pain. That capacity comes from having learned to experience frustration; the frustration of our deprivation in childhood, which had to be adequate enough to have curbed our narcissism.

Without feelings, there is no love. Without loving, there is no sharing. Without sharing, the world as we know it will cease to exist.

If the macho man continues to have his way, he will "stay cool," remain "laid back," and won't let himself "get hassled." In other words, he won't let himself get caught up in feeling.

How do we help people to feel? Feelings lie at the very heart of the irrational part of man that we have been unable to educate. Is mankind locked into a closed system, or is there a way out?

The discovery of the unconscious was a major breakthrough in understanding the irrational nature of man. For the first time he was able to focus on his more primitive, biologically anchored drives. New insights into the dynamics of human motivation emerged from the work of such men as Freud, Jung, and Adler. Through their studies, our irrational dreams, slips of the tongue, and unintended acts could be understood. Reasons were discovered for what had previously been regarded as illogical behavior. These insights offered a new dimension of thought that could be applied to human education.

Unfortunately, its application was destined to be

reserved for a special few. The psychoanalytic movement evolved into an elitist group who claimed an
exclusive right to psychoanalytic theory. They established training institutions outside the boundaries of
organized education. They limited their teachings to
small, select groups and isolated themselves from the
general public. They explained their seclusive behavior
in terms of the need to protect the purity of their ideas.

Thus, psychoanalysts virtually left the responsibility
for bringing knowledge of the unconscious to the educational system in the hands of marginally competent
people who have oversimplified the complex psychoanalytic ideas. Where truths about the irrational nature
of man could have broadened the dimensions of learning, half-truths have constricted them. Nevertheless,
the analysts have remained on the sidelines as aloof
critics rather than as active participants. They chose to
confine their efforts at educating the public to psychoanalytic therapy, which is a highly expensive process
in terms of time, energy, and money, and is available
only to a handful of people.

Psychoanalysis has the potential to serve the greater
good of man by helping all of us deal with the irrational components of our being. It is the first educational experience that deals directly with our capacity
for loving. Indeed, success in psychoanalytic treatment
is measured in terms of growth in the ability to love.
It is designed to elaborate feelings in the service of increasing one's trust for another human being.

Now, as never before, there is a need to dedicate ourselves to a massive new commitment to education. Not
merely by increasing the number of schools or by add-
ing new subjects to an existing core curriculum, which
has already failed our society, but by shifting our educational focus from the rational to the irrational, from
knowing to loving.

As many people as possible must be educated about
their own basic nature. A whole new frame of edu-

cational reference must be evolved, a concept of education that replaces the emphasis on intellect with an emphasis on man's feelings. It would require the incorporation of psychoanalytic insights into the structure of public education.

In this regard, the theoretical differences among psychoanalysts are secondary to their common concern about feelings and the dynamics of unconscious motivation. In terms of public education, we need not specifically commit ourselves to the ideas of Freud vs. Sullivan vs. Horney vs. Reich vs. Klein vs. Jung vs. Rado—and so on. We can make use of their communal thinking about the relevance of feelings and the means to achieve fuller expression of them while adapting to socially inhibiting forces.

The classroom experience would become more than a situation in which mechanical learning takes place. It would become an ongoing group seminar for self-awareness. For example, in learning about the refraction of light, personal values would be stressed. Instead of emphasis on the fact that the angle of incidence equals the angle of refraction, children would deal with the subject of light as it relates to such things as the hazard of driving at sunset, the effect of the placement of light on their appearance, and the effect of reflected sunlight on heating or cooling their houses. In this regard, instead of only facts being communicated, feelings about light would be explored.

A unique opportunity is available today to restructure education. The very technology that came from training our rational qualities has produced new means to educate us about our irrationality. The new dimensions of audio-visual communication are mind-boggling. The proliferation of cable television, satellite transmission, and video discs and cassettes offers ways of reaching the individual on levels never available before.

This dramatic breakthrough in audio-visual communication is particularly relevant to training the irrational aspects of our behavior. Traditionally, man has had great difficulty in altering deeply ingrained personal values through education. Efforts by schools to change prejudicial attitudes—ranging from the conviction that only whole wheat bread has nutrient value to ethnic generalizations spouting that all blacks have rhythm, all Poles are stupid, all Jews are grasping—have always failed. There was no effective route to travel from the rational to the irrational until the work of Piaget and others demonstrated that the more sensory modalities that are brought to bear on a learning experience, the greater is the potential for reaching irrational levels of human behavior.

In the past, education has relied almost entirely on language in order to communicate. Language is a highly sophisticated form of behavior that requires reason and the capacity for abstraction. But it is the most ineffective tool for reaching the unreasonable qualities of man; it is too dependent on logical order. The more primitive modalities of sight, touch, and smell are far more capable of reaching the more irrational—and more primitive—levels of our behavior.

Modern technology makes communication possible with emphasis on the more pervasive sense of sight; the use of sound only secondarily; words could supplement visual images, in contrast to the past, when visual aids were used to supplement words. Moreover, the presentation of information to students will be possible on greatly improved levels. The ideas of the best creative minds in the world would be directly available to children on film, tape, and video disc. The ideas themselves could be dramatized through the use of special effects, animation, and by personalities interesting to children. Learning would become fun. The format of *Sesame Street* could be extended and developed to cover the whole range of educational programming from kindergarten to graduate school and from the nursery to evening adult classes.

The teacher would no longer function primarily as a source of information, but as someone concerned almost exclusively with how that information could be made useful to each individual in the class. Students would get the information at home, before coming to class, from prerecorded video cassettes and discs; a slow learner could replay them as often as it proved necessary for him to grasp the material. The classroom would then become a place of applied learning rather than factual learning. From the beginning of each school day, the teacher could focus the attention of the class on the meaning of the prelearned information and the feelings the students have about it. The school curriculum would be able to emphasize feelings over facts.

We are running out of time. We have no choice about such an undertaking. We must develop better means to learn to love.

In order for an educational rededication to be possible, it is absolutely vital that we first redefine and drastically change the professional status of our teachers. Presently, teachers occupy the low end of the professional hierarchy. They are among the lowest paid and require the least amount of formal training. Consequently, teaching does not attract our most talented people.

Teachers should be our most talented professionals and the most highly regarded—the highest-paid—members of our society. The responsibility for maintaining the meaningfulness of our lives is theirs.

Up until now, by selectively rewarding the lawyer, doctor, engineer, architect, and media celebrities with privileges and wealth far in excess of those given to the teacher, we have committed ourselves to the support of narcissism. These professionals protect our rights, safeguard our health, build our castles, and entertain us. They certainly have a role to fulfill, but the extent to which we allow them to dominate our value system reveals our self-centeredness.

The teacher is the specialist in providing loving. We have all but abandoned him and what he represents. We take pride in the American tradition of free education, but we don't hesitate to quickly prune the school budget in response to inflation and the increasing cost of government. Still we go on spending everywhere else—buying bigger and better cars, dining at the best restaurants—in spite of the increase in prices. Everywhere, that is, except in our schools.

It seems that to support narcissism, no price is too high to pay. To support loving through education, almost any price appears to be too high.

There is an alternative; to dedicate ourselves to a new era in education based on our technology. Our greatest minds can provide a learning forum for all of us. Education can become the province of the best of our professionals.

The opportunity to create a more loving world is here. We have only to turn away from our narcissistic preferences and commit ourselves to our survival as a viable society.

15 /

It's Your Choice

The issues are clear. Either we continue our ever-increasing narcissistic pursuits, or we commit ourselves to loving. It is a choice that each of us must make individually, but it affects all of us collectively.

It is not an easy choice. Our natural inclinations point us toward narcissism, and narcissism has much to offer—instant gratification of every variety and type of desire; freedom from responsibility for others, accompanied by the right to be dependent on others; a life built exclusively around our own needs and self-survival, and the pursuit of limitless powers. This is pretty hard stuff to resist.

Loving, on the other hand, is not a natural inclination. It is an ability that has to be learned and cultivated. Its origins lie in man's determination to survive through social living. Within the framework of restrictions that are an inevitable consequence of society, loving is the best means of finding pleasure. The pleasures it provides are of the most enduring kind.

The pleasures obtained from loving cannot match the moment-to-moment intensity of narcissistic highs, but they do protect us from the recurrent cycle of desperate lows that are an invariable part of narcissism.

In order to be able to love, however, great personal discipline and emotional strength are required. Loving cannot exist unless we are willing to expose ourselves to the vulnerability that accompanies the expression of feelings. That is hard work.

The narcissist works hard, too, but only to extract the good life without having to deal with the consequences. He must always have some loving people around him to feed off. Once he gets them to love him, their need to give enables him to take without giving as much in return. He shares only his superficial charm and style, and receives in return their commitment of love, support, and care.

Loving people are easy marks. The narcissist takes from them and discards them when they are no longer useful to him. He sets up one-way relationships in which others care about him and he is free to care only for himself. He is able to manipulate loving people through the feelings of guilt that inevitably accompany the ability to love. But he is not accessible to manipulation, because he lacks the conscience necessary in order to feel guilty.

It is loving people who provide the narcissist with the means of sustaining his narcissism. If the narcissist were to live only among other narcissists, his plight would be desperate. There would be no one to extract caring from, no one to charm and consume. There would be only mirror images of himself, a crowd of other narcissists, all of whom also seek to live only for themselves.

In such a purely narcissistic society there is no room for interdependence. Everyone must fend for himself. It is exclusively a kill-or-be-killed world. Survival is possible only as long as one remains the fittest.

This is not the way of life a narcissist really wants. He wants the privileges of self-indulgence that accrue to the fittest in a world where everything is for the taking, while at the same time he is provided with the protection and security given to the least fit in a world where the weak must be cared for. What he wants is the best of both worlds. It's a hell of a trick if he can pull it off, but in order for him to succeed, it will take some "loving patsies" who are willing to pay his prices for him.

Strange as it may seem, there are more and more loving volunteers available to pick up the narcissist's dues for living. Since the ability to love is never a totally pure one, the narcissist holds some attraction for all of us in that he is free of the very restraints and feelings of guilt that characterize the loving state. That is, the narcissist provides vicarious outlets for our own suppressed, natural, and constantly available narcissistic interests. The more narcissistic we are, the greater is our attraction for narcissists.

We become more willing to act as foils for a narcissist because that serves our purposes as well. We look to act out our own feelings of specialness and our self-centered interest in pleasure through him, trying to hide our narcissism behind his, while posing as the innocent victims of his selfishness.

Relationships built around narcissism to service common narcissistic needs will last only as long as the illusion of love is permitted to persist. This requires that the more loving partner give of himself to the more narcissistic one under the guise of caring. If, on the other hand, the narcissistic desires of both partners are brought into the open, the binding mystique of the relationship is lost. The more narcissistic of the two is particularly disenchanted; he rejects in the other what he reserves for himself. The ground rules entitle only one at a time to live with narcissistic privileges surrounded by loving.

In my experience, this is one of the most common reasons why marriages break up. Time and time again I encounter couples who are too angry to go on living together because the narcissistic demands of one marital partner have either used up or overwhelmed the other's.

For example, an actress who had failed at two previous marriages with men in the entertainment field wanted to protect herself from a third failure due to narcissism. She consciously decided to find a husband who would not be caught up with the feelings of specialness that are so often a part of being in show business; one who would be able to devote himself to her. So she married a warm, giving businessman who had maintained a low profile throughout his life.

It was not long, however, before he became her business manager and was deeply ensconced in her career. Instead of bringing friends from the world outside show business to his wife, he took up almost exclusively with her acquaintances from the world of entertainment and abandoned his previous identity. The narcissistic opportunities provided by her work gave him the means to ventilate his own narcissism. Instead of broadening the parameters of her life through his love, he constricted the loving dimensions of his life by expressing his narcissism through hers.

This was a man whose narcissism would have remained better contained if he had not entered into the marriage. That statement is not meant to imply that his actress wife was responsible for his narcissism. It only reflects the reality that if narcissistic input is high enough, anyone is vulnerable. The most loving and best adjusted among us would have difficulty navigating the glamour and excitement of show business.

Each time a relationship between a more loving person and a narcissist breaks up, it moves the narcissist further into his narcissistic life style. That is not a great loss to our society. Unfortunately, however, it also drives the more loving partner into a more narcissistic way of life, because his ability to trust has been diminished. That is a serious loss to our society.

At the rate that loving is disappearing from our world, we can ill afford to lose out on any of our collective capacity to care.

Restraining narcissism is the key to loving. It makes life an endless series of difficult choices for a loving person. The choices are always between the conflicting needs of narcissistic self-love and loving others. To decide in favor of loving others always requires the denial of some form of narcissistic self-interest.

Each of us thinks he can tolerate just a bit more narcissism without losing control of the craving. Like an alcoholic looking for just one more drink, or the junkie for just one more fix, the loving person keeps reaching for just one more high. Unfortunately, such is the insidious nature of narcissism that we can never be sure of the moment at which we stop being able to control it, and it starts to control us. So if we want to remain more loving, we must lean to the more conservative choices, err on the side of underestimating our control rather than overestimating it.

It is time for us to be vulnerable again. It is time to risk expressing our feelings and sharing them. It is time to stop wasting our care on those who couldn't care less. It is time to be real, first to ourselves and then to others. It is time to reject the façade of false glitter, superficial imagery, and the promise of higher and higher highs. It is time to stop glorifying and indulging celebrities with rewards in excess of their worth.

Look out for that hunger inside you that longs to be special. Look out for the person on the outside who tells you he can make you special.

Whether you like it or not, you must constantly be aware that it is impossible to be special. You can be better at some things than at others, but you're never above the battle. Every time your need to fool yourself into believing that you are special allows somebody to sell you, or you to sell yourself, the "right" car, the "right" restaurant, the "right" house in the "right" neighborhood, the "right" label in your clothes, the "right" people as friends, or the "right" way to live, you're a loser—and you make the rest of us losers, too.

So how do we protect ourselves from becoming losers? How do we handle our own narcissism? How do we decide how much of it each of us can tolerate without becoming subordinated to it? Are there signs that help us recognize the cutoff point?

It would be wonderful if at this juncture I could come up with a clear set of guidelines, a list of "do's" and "dont's" that would protect us from going too far while at the same time enabling us to go far enough. I would very much like to, but I can't. No such list exists.

There is no clean line that separates narcissistic behavior from more loving behavior. Since all behavior is motivated by a multiplicity of factors, no act is pure enough to provide clear-cut signals of the point at which loving stops and narcissism begins. These forces overlap and intermingle with one another.

The line "I love you because of what I feel when I am with you" is both narcissistic and loving in meaning. It is loving in that it reports the shared feelings communicated from one lover to another. On the other hand, it can be narcissistically interpreted to describe what one lover takes from the other.

The answer can be found only within the person who wrote the words in the first place. He alone can decipher the maze of feelings in such a statement and issue is not decided in terms of whether loving feelings or narcissistic feelings exist; they always exist. It is a question of which ones dominate.

I help a blind man across the street. I do it because therefore determine which of his motives prevail. The it makes me feel better that I am able to see. I do it because it will make others think of me as a more considerate and kind person. I do it out of real concern

186

for the blind man's ability to cross safely by himself. I do it seeking no reward other than that of being helpful to him. So why do I really do it? Certainly for all the reasons I described. But one will take precedence over all the others. If I honestly explore my motives, I can know for the most part whether I did it for him or for myself.

For all of us, the answer can be found only in ourselves. It is safe to assume that both loving and narcissism are present in everything we do. Only by exploring the motives that contribute to our behavior can we decide which of the two is primary.

We should be equally discerning about the powerful outside forces of narcissism—the media, for instance. We can use it to fill the void in our lives, as a passive way of being entertained. We can allow it to make decisions for us—tell us whom to vote for, how to dress, eat, walk, talk, and live. We can allow it to stop us from reading. We can even allow it to think for us, whenever possible. Or we can always be discerning and vigilant about not permitting it to undermine our personal autonomy. We can try to make sure that it does not dominate us. We can work to prevent it from manipulating us. We can even control the rate at which it will proliferate.

If we don't watch television shows that aren't worth watching, they will no longer be telecast. If we don't pay money to see movies that aren't worth seeing, they will no longer be produced. The studios and networks are not really in control; we are. But only if we take the time and expend the effort to exercise our individual preferences.

If we cop out and go to a movie because there is nothing better to do, rather than because the film is worth seeing, we forfeit our self-assertive rights. If we turn on the television set in order to avoid conversation, rather than because there is something specific we want to see, we once again forfeit our self-assertive rights.

Every time we forfeit our self-assertive rights, the media will assume them for us. We contribute to its growth by our own forfeiture—and underwrite the ludicrous salaries of media celebrities at a time when education can barely sustain itself.

Each time we encounter violence, there are a number of factors we must be aware of: if we don't actively resist it because it's happening to the next guy and not to us, then we're supporting it; if we don't actively resist it because we're too afraid of retaliation, then we're supporting it; if we encourage violence as a means of problem solving, then we are advocating it, whether it occurs on the streets of New York or in the jungles of Vietnam.

Every time we buy toy guns, toy knives, or Kung Fu chains for our children, we are training them to live with violence. Every time we support movies, books, television shows, or newscasts that excessively portray violence, we ingrain violence more deeply into our lives. Every time we encourage our children to expect fulfillment of all their demands, we are preparing them to be violent.

If we want too much from life, we will become violent when we are disappointed. The violence in us may not be directly expressed, but it will be felt by those close to us. The greater the reservoir of unexpressed violence becomes, the greater the potential for its expression by others. Angry feelings inside ourselves reinforces the anger in others.

We cannot expect others to control our violence for us. They can only assist us to control it ourselves. If we can learn to want less, we won't be so angry so much of the time.

In considering marriage, we should be aware that, first and foremost, it is ideally a relationship entered into by choice, an independent action undertaken by an independent human being. It is compromised if it is a relationship formed by two dependent people to protect themselves from their insecurity.

When two independent people who don't need each other choose to live together because they want each other, they have the beginnings of a good marriage. But only the beginnings. To develop and sustain the relationship requires hard work. Time and effort devoted to maintaining the qualities that make a marriage a good one cannot be reserved for birthdays, Christmas, and Valentine's Day; they must be invested and reinvested every day.

In a good marriage, the marital partners are very good friends. They trust each other. They feel free to expose themselves to each other, secure in the knowledge that neither will exploit the other's vulnerabilities. Consequently, they are able to communicate well with each other—not just share information and ideas, but also feelings. Communicative interaction is never satisfactory until some expression of feeling is exchanged.

The intimacy of the communication between the partners is never greater than when they are making love. Lovemaking is an expression of intimate communication for them. They communicate with every one of the senses that contributes to the human dimension. They touch, taste, smell, and see, as well as talk to each other. They try to avoid sexual play that is technical and mechanistic, aware that every time they sell out their commitment to communicate in the service of "getting it on," they compromise their relationship. What makes a marriage work well is communicative compatibility. It must be preserved above everything else.

The good marriage is spiced with romance, which is a reflection of narcissism. It heightens and supports the excitement of the relationship, the moments of elation that buffer the constant sobering impact of reality. Romance carries with it fantasy and illusion, a little of which goes a long way. Excessive need for fantasy and illusion is a signal that the marriage as a real relationship is no longer working.

The most fragile component of a good marriage is the romance it provides. The harsh, competitive realities of everyday life constantly threaten to destroy romance. The demands of physically providing for each other, for instance, can become overly consuming. But the most serious threat comes from the intrusive demands of having a family.

The decision to bring a child into the marriage is a very serious one, because a child irreversibly changes the relationship. There is less time and less freedom for romance. Children are omnipresent forces, and raising them demands a great deal of work from parents. The energies invested in children detract from what was previously invested only in the partners. The presence of children, however, can also bring balance and stability. Children provide a sobering influence on the narcissism of the parents.

Once children are present, an intimate relationship of marriage shared only by two willing partners shifts to become a family involving three or more partners, not all of whom are necessarily willing participants. Initially, the child is an outsider to the very relationship that created him. During the course of his growth, he can come to dominate the family and subordinate the parents' interests in each other to their common concerns for him. If he succeeds in doing this, everybody loses. If he fails to establish a child-centered home, then everybody can win. The parents can retain the primacy of their loving relationship and the child will be forced into the ultimately benefiting pattern of more independent development.

The key to the good marriage and to good family living is independence. Excessive dependency causes a marriage to become a relationship whose bonds arise out of fear of being alone, rather than out of the desire to share.

The dependent person cannot communicate honestly. He is too weak to trust others. He has to protect himself from exposure, so he adopts images to mask his vulnerability. Not surprisingly, his limited ability to communicate intrudes upon his lovemaking. It requires him to become more proficient in sexual techniques in order to compensate for the feeling void. He makes his greatest fear come true; his fear of being alone ultimately drives him to be lonely, even in the presence of others. His constant need to protect himself deprives him of any opportunity to let another come to know him as he truly is.

An important part of loving is being able to let go. But dependent people cannot let go; they need others too much, and this limits their capacity for pleasure through loving.

We all know when we are permitting ourselves to lean on others. No matter what façade we assume—whether it be the macho man or the liberated woman —we are aware when our gestures of independence are not real. The bottom line is not measured in terms of what we can get others to think about us, but in terms of what we know of ourselves.

If we know ourselves as dependent human beings, there are prices we will have to pay in life as a result of our need to get others to carry our load for us. We will be less able to love, less able to express feelings, less willing to make choices in living. We will be more interested in manipulating others than in freeing them, in holding on to them than in letting them go. Our inability to find pleasure in loving and sexual communication will make us more vulnerable to narcissism. So we will seek power and material possessions far in excess of our needs. We will seek immortality by self-perpetuation. In every way it will be hard to "live and let live"; you cannot let others live unless you have a fulfilling life of your own.

Autonomy and loving go hand in hand. Self-sufficient, independent people who are willing to carry their own weight are able to share. To the extent that they share, they limit the expression of narcissism in their lives.

Dependency and narcissism go hand in hand. Dependent, manipulative people do not share; they need. To the extent that they do not share, they increase the expression of narcissism in their lives.

Each of us knows when he is leaning on others, manipulating them to serve his own ends. Each of us knows when he is acting. Each of us knows when he is feeling. Each of us knows when he is unwilling to share what he feels. Each of us knows when he cares about someone else—and when he is merely pretending to care.

None of us is totally free of dependency, manipulation, acting, being uncaring, being unwilling to share, grasping for power—narcissism in any of its reflected glories. The differences among us are relative. What is critical is the nature of the forces that are predominant in our lives. Many forces can exist, but only one can dominate at a time.

Paying the price for *choosing* to love is the core of the issue. To the extent that we are narcissists, we are bargain hunters. We want to get something for nothing; we seek to avoid having to give up anything important to us. But if you can't give up things, you'll never be able to make the choices that loving requires.

In this book, I have tried to trace the development of narcissism in our society. In the time of the earliest human existence on earth, the struggle to survive served to protect our loving qualities; the need for interdependence and mutual support was crucial. The occasional narcissist was tolerated because the overwhelming majority was by necessity committed to loving. Consequently, society was able to prevail. Indeed, it flourished.

As society continued to flourish, some people accumulated sufficient material supplies so that, for them, survival was no longer an issue. At first they were few, but their numbers grew. They were the beginning of a privileged class, people who employed others to provide for them. Not just for sustenance, but for pleasure as well.

Today they are no longer the few, but the many. In the wake of a social affluence man has never previously achieved, an entire middle class has grown to become privileged. Its numbers are so great that there are not enough others to provide for their sustenance and pleasure.

Affluence itself is not to blame, but rather our inability to accommodate ourselves to it. A high standard of living does not erode a society, it enhances it—but only as long as the society's members maintain their commitment to one another—loving.

To live better does not intrude upon caring. But to believe we're unduly special because we live better does intrude, because exaggerated feelings of specialness and narcissism go hand in hand.

Our forefathers left us room to grow as a society. It is not growth that threatens us, but the manner in which we grow. If enough of us no longer contribute to society because we have been provided for by our birthright, then the basic nature of society will change, shifting from a collective effort to a struggle between the takers and the givers. The takers will have their feast, the givers will get stuck with the check—and the price gets higher every day. It will go on this way until the bill becomes unpayable because the majority of us will have become takers. Ultimately, the system will collapse.

The takers of the world are the narcissists. The givers of the world are the loving people. The balance between the two determines the quality of social life. As society becomes more and more narcissistic, loving people are progressively eliminated. They suffocate from an inability to find others with whom they can communicate intimately. Their feelings are consumed by the uncaring people around them. There is not enough interdependence to maintain the structure of a functioning society, and they are left unprotected from the violence of asocial narcissists.

The turbulence in our society reflects the precarious balance between narcissists and loving people. We are getting closer to the point of no return all the time. This is the moment of decision.

Our society can no longer afford the luxury of taking care of its narcissists. There are too many. It has to take care of those who can still love. There are too few.

It's our choice, one that each and every one of us will make in one form or another—consciously or unconsciously, sooner or later.

If enough of us choose narcissism, there will be no other alternative for the rest. Society as we know it will no longer exist.

So, whatever the outcome of your life may be, blame no one but yourself; it will be a result of the choice you will have made.

I, for one, would like us to maintain a more loving way of life. But none of us can do it alone. We need to help each other while there's still time.

Let us make a commitment to help each other to love more and in that way keep our narcissism under control. Before it's too late.